THE BEST
BIKE RIDES
IN
CALIFORNIA

THE BEST BIKE RIDES IN CALIFORNIA

by

Kimberly Grob

A Voyager Book

The Globe Pequot Press

Old Saybrook, Connecticut

Photos by Kimberly Grob, Kevin Lee, and Casey Mahone

Library of Congress Cataloging-in-Publication Data

Grob, Kimberly.
  The best bike rides in California / by Kimberly Grob. — 1st ed.
       p.   cm.
  "A Voyager book."
  ISBN 1-56440-527-3
  1. Bicycle touring—California—Guidebooks. 2. California—Guidebooks.
I. Title.
GV1045.5.C2G75   1995
796.6'4'09794—dc20
                                                            94-38532
                                                            CIP

♻ This text and cover are printed on recycled paper.
Manufactured in the United States of America
First Edition/Second Printing

To Kevin,

For always telling me I'm looking strong on long mountain climbs. Even when I'm ready to puke, topple over, or drop dead from exhaustion, you are always my faithful cheerleader.

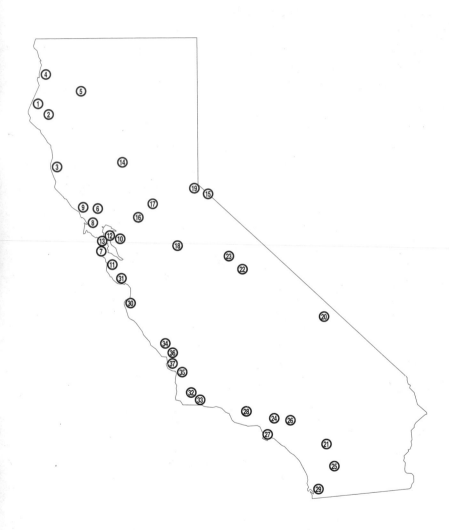

Contents

Acknowledgments ix

Introduction 1

How to Use This Book 3
Getting the Most out of Your Ride 4

Bike Rides 7

Upper North 7
San Francisco Bay Area 35
Gold Country/Cascades/Lake Tahoe 79
Mountains and Desert 111
Southern California 131
Central Coast 161

Appendixes 201

Regional Cycling Magazines 202
Recommended Reading 203
Cycling Maps 204
On-Line Information 204
Cycling Clubs 204

Acknowledgments

This book could never have been written without the guidance and encouragement I've received from family, friends, industry peers, and, often, strangers. Thanks to my first editor at *California Bicyclist*, Dale Butler, for getting me involved in this highly addictive sport, and to Phrancis Falcone for taking me on my first real ride. Thanks also to *California Bicyclist*'s Henry Kingman for sharing his abundant knowledge of California backroads and for recommending me for this book project. Furthermore, I'm grateful to Nancy Vierra, Sheri Pepper, and Linda Rosek for allowing me the flexibility in my part-time job to get this project completed. And I'm forever grateful to my parents and my sisters, Jennifer and Amy, for their sympathetic ears, to all my close friends who have been neglected during the writing of this book, and to Kevin Lee for accompanying me on many a road ride when he would have preferred to be somewhere else.

Many cyclists have contributed rides to this book. Some of them are friends that merely took me on a mind-blowing ride years back, never knowing it would one day be incorporated in a book. Others are acquaintances and strangers who've been willing to share some of their favorite rides specifically for this book. Those cyclists include Ernst Wilhelm, Stefan Klakovich, Dale Butler, Henry Kingman, Barbara Hanscome, Andrew Christensen, Chris Kostman, Bob Winning, Ed McLaughlin, Patrick Owens, Monica Pappas, Kathy Enquist, Joe Zoellin, and Larry Tubbs. Thanks also to many helpful strangers who pointed me in the right direction and gave me a helping hand out on the road in times of trouble. If you ride your bike long enough, you will learn that there are plenty of Good Samaritans left in the world. Thanks to all of them, whose names I never got the chance to learn.

Introduction

*Ride your bike, even if it fails to draw admiring glances at
the post-ride cafe. Even if the self you see in your fantasies
wouldn't be seen on it. The ride's the thing.*
—Maynard Hershon, *California Bicyclist*

When you're nine years old, bicycling isn't a route slip and a map,
and it certainly isn't a titanium stem or hand-built wheels. It's a
blur of colors. A rush of wind. A feeling of freedom. Kids don't
need much of anything to enjoy the sport, except their own self-
reliance and thirst for adventure. It's a time in life when riding is as
pure as it gets. But eventually we grow up and things get more
complicated. We buy nicer bikes. We buy touring books.

In 1976 I entered my first bicycle race. Freckled and flat-chested
and toothpick-legged, I shoved my way up to the front of the start
line with the older boys. As the start drew near, my legs twitched
with nervous energy. My face flushed hot with anxiety. Six miles
through the subdivision to the swimming pool and back. I'd done
it a million times. One-handed. No-handed. Pedaling with Sheryl
Mixon on the seat and Little Lynn on the handlebars. I could do it
now. And I could win. Because I was nine and I was a girl and I
knew how strong I was; the anvil of gender hadn't yet been
dropped on me.

The race started, and I spun glorious, joyous, girlish pedalstrokes
amid the neighborhood boys twice my age. But little more than
100 yards from the start line, my glory ride ended in a heap of
metal and tears and twisted limbs. A boy—out of control in the
frenzy of competition—barreled into me, abruptly finishing the
ride for both of us.

I didn't think about bikes again for thirteen years, and it was
seventeen years before I tried another race. Instead, I busied myself
with the normal girl things. I took gymnastics and ballet. I wrote
boys' names on my Trapper Keeper. I went to the prom. I went to

college. I grew up to be a Very Nice Girl. And while there was almost always a bike in my life during those years, I don't remember any of them; they were either gathering dust in a garage or getting rusted in the rain.

I remember instead a blue bike with fenders, ordered for me from the Sears catalog: the dented, rattling, squeaky steed of my ill-fated ride of 1976. I remember my pride in the "Spirit of '76" logo I stenciled on the chain guard with red spray paint, just to be fancy. And I remember the giddy rush of riding as fast as I could through soft, wooded dirt on early summer mornings. Cars and houses and neighborhood kids gone, I was a little girl alone, zooming past tall, damp trees. And it was frightening and fun and free.

That bike must've cost my parents $50, tops. It was just a cheap, department-store thing. It wasn't for racing, and it wasn't for mountain biking. But I didn't know that, so on it I did both. On it I rode like a little girl who hasn't yet learned to be prissy. Like any reckless kid—boy or girl—who hasn't discovered fear. Fear of accidents, insurance premiums, and equipment. Fear of having a bike that's too heavy, too cheap, too ugly, too embarrassing—generally not right.

My Spirit of '76 bike is long gone. But even now, sometimes, when everything is going right and I'm riding strong and confident and energetic, that giddy, girlish feeling I used to get when I mounted the Spirit of '76 comes back to me. For a moment the fears of adulthood are washed away, not by titanium or clipless pedals or acro bars but by the unfathomable beauty of a California ridge, the wind in my face on a coasty, twisty descent, or the pure, breathless exhaustion of an all-out sprint—whether racing against strangers or on a bike path with friends.

Use this book as a tool to help you get to that place—if only for a moment—where bicycling is as good and pure as it was when you were a kid. You can be a formidable racer, or you can be slower than your grandpa on his John Deere tractor; your bike can cost a conservative $200, or it can cost a cool $2,000. But if you're out there riding long enough, it'll get you there. And it won't matter that you have a mortgage payment due and an insurance policy to worry about. Or that your bike doesn't sport the latest gadget. For the moment, all that will matter is that you're on your bike and you're alive and you're lucky enough to be riding in California, one of the most dramatic and diverse states in all of America.

Enjoy the rides!

How to Use This Book

Think of this book as an old, weathered cycling friend. The one who's been around the proverbial block more than a few times. This buddy of yours will take you on a sampling of its favorite rides, but in the long run you'll find your own variations of these, and you'll come up with your own list of favorites.

By all means, branch out! This book is not a bible; it's merely a starting point, a launching pad for your own adventures. It's meant to be a trusty resource, an accurate, reliable guide, and a faithful friend. But those who get the most out of its pages will be those who are bold enough to build upon the book's suggestions.

For starters, each time you embark on one of these rides, it's a good idea to carry a road map of the area in addition to the map appearing in this book. That way you'll be able to navigate around unexpected road construction, get yourself out of a pickle if you become totally lost, and discover new roads to ride. There are some great cycling-specific maps produced by Krebs Cycle Products that highlight scenic roads and make it easy to chart your own routes and find those elusive backroads. (For more information on this and other resources, see the Appendixes in the back of this book.)

In order to arm you with the knowledge you'll need to get the most out of this book, every ride is rated to reflect its degree of difficulty.

Rambles are the gentlest rides, perfect for the beginning cyclist or for riders looking for a relaxed outing. All rambles are less than 30 miles long and cover flat or rolling terrain.

Cruises are intermediate-level rides, ranging in length from 25 to 60 miles. They include rolling hills and sometimes a major climb.

Challenges require more experience. Beginning riders who take on challenges may find themselves cursing the road, this book, and life in general about halfway through the ride. These routes are tough. They're often longer than 60 miles. They always include major climbs. They make your legs hurt.

Classics are the most difficult rides in the book and are most suitable for experienced riders. They are usually more than 75 miles, sometimes more than 100, and they always include tough climbs. Tackle them at your own risk, and don't say I didn't warn you!

The rating system is designed to help you choose rides that are appropriate for your experience level, riding style, and mood for the day. Feel like trying to lure your nonbikie friend into the sport? An ultrascenic ramble may be just the ticket. Experiencing the need to hammer your brains out and restate your virility? There are classics in here that could frighten even the most bad-assed, big-legged bike fanatics around. Of course, most of the rides are somewhere in between these two extremes, and many of them are doable by just about anyone. So take these ratings as suggestions, and try not to get too hung up on the definitions. A ramble may seem more like a classic to a beginner, and the real toughsters out there may laugh at some of the rides I call challenges.

Getting the Most out of Your Ride

Think of all the cyclo-journalists out there who have penned articles, papers, and books on our many-faceted sport. Just on the subject of smart and safe riding techniques, stacks of articles and books have been written. And while collecting and absorbing written advice can improve your riding tremendously, it's the miles in the saddle that really make the cyclist. Learning to ride intelligently— and to ride with grace, etiquette, and class—is a continual process of education and experience. It seems there's always more to learn.

Cyclo-journalists and their cycling advice have been around since the invention of two wheels. There is, however, at least a common thread in their teachings. The following cycling credo was developed in the late 1800s by a respected writer and rider named Velocio (Paul de Vivie). It covers all the basics and is as relevant today as it was then.

Velocio's Commandments

1. Stop briefly and not too often, so as not to chill or lose your rhythm.
2. Eat frequently and lightly, eat before you are hungry, and drink before you are thirsty.
3. Don't push yourself until you're too tired to eat or sleep.
4. Add clothing before you are cold, take it off before you are hot, but don't avoid sun, air, and rain.
5. Avoid alcohol and meat, at least while on the road.
6. Ride within your limits. Learn your pace, and don't be tempted to force yourself during the first hours of a ride, when you are fresh.
7. Don't show off (ride out of vanity).

To this I add a 1990s addendum: Always wear a helmet.

For more cycling resources that'll move you forward in your quest to be a safe and smart rider, check out the Appendixes in the back of this book.

Disclaimer

The Globe Pequot Press assumes no liability for accidents happening to, or injuries sustained by, readers who engage in the activities described in this book.

Upper North

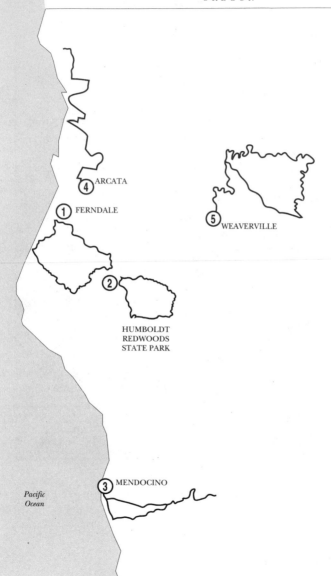

OREGON

④ ARCATA

① FERNDALE

② HUMBOLDT
REDWOODS
STATE PARK

⑤ WEAVERVILLE

③ MENDOCINO

Pacific
Ocean

Upper North

1. Lost Coast Classic 10

2. Dyerville Loop Challenge 15

3. Comptche Cruise 20

4. Patrick's Point Cruise 24

5. Trinity Alps Challenge 29

1

Lost Coast Classic

Ferndale—Scotia—Avenue of the Giants—Honeydew—
Petrolia—Lost Coast—Capetown—Ferndale

> *After 80 miles, if the road rises at all, it rises near-vertically.*
> *At least once, no matter how long you've been riding, you'll*
> *reach for low gear as eagerly as a drowning man reaches for*
> *a lifesaving rope—and already be in it. Gulp.*
> —Maynard Hershon, *California Bicyclist*

Hanging precipitously on the edge of California, the Lost Coast is like a chaste beauty living in an ivory tower. Despite its eye-popping splendor, the inaccessibilty of the land locks it into virtual anonymity. When Highway 101 turns inward at Legget, it takes with it the majority of auto-addicted tourists. Only the most intrepid of travelers, the ones who can handle not having a major highway or city anywhere nearby, make it to the isolated shores of the Lost Coast. Because of this, the area is ideal for cycling. The secluded backroads that make up this ride range from dense, dark redwood groves to a jagged coastline of black-sand beaches stretching out to meet the Pacific Ocean.

The ride takes you almost 75 miles before your wheels actually roll onto the Lost Coast road. For the sake of convenience, the ride starts at an accessible locale and gets progressively "lost" with every mile. The Victorian hamlet of Ferndale, which boasts painted-lady homes and elegant storefronts decorated in pastels and fancy trim work, is the starting point for the ride. The town's ornamental charm is in ultimate contrast to the unrestrained beauty of the Lost Coast.

This route is patterned after the annual Tour of the Unknown Coast century ride, which is touted as one of California's toughest centuries. And after eight miles of cycling, you'll get a taste of what you're in for when you encounter your first big hill en route to Rio Dell. From here, it's a short ride to Scotia, a town almost completely owned by Pacific Lumber Company. This lumber empire extends from one end of town to the other, and when you finally roll to the end of it, you'll turn onto Highway 101S.

As you pedal onto Highway 101, your ability to measure your progress in small chunks from city to city all but disappears. After nearly six miles, you'll leave the rush of cars behind and greet the ancient redwoods as you pedal onto the famed Avenue of the Giants. The soft, dank shelter of these towering trees yields a mossy carpet of forest floor, with mushrooms sprouting everywhere in a wild, mutating frenzy.

Your route tumbles deeper into the secluded world of nature as you turn onto Bull Creek Road and begin a gentle, quiet climb through the redwoods. The road is a pastoral poem where sheep roam freely, often holding court right in the middle of the road.

When you reach the tiny town of Honeydew, at mile 55.6, you'll find a store where you can re-fuel and chill out for awhile. From here, country roads transport you through the town of Petrolia and finally deposit you at the Lost Coast. And it is here, at mile 73, that much hardship awaits.

At the coast, gusty winds laced with sand can drop your cruising speed down to less than 10 mph. Cattle wandering aimlessly along the road provide that obstacle-course element so often missing in other rides. And then there's The Wall. At mile 81.5, your wind-beaten limbs will be forced to attack a one-mile, 18 percent grade. And right after you've recovered from that, you'll be faced with the Endless Hill, thrown in for good measure at mile 86.7, just to ensure that you've really worked for your 100 miles. After 85 miles of pedaling, a bump on the road can seem endless—and this 8-mile climb ain't no bump.

Just remember, when you reach the summit, you're finally

home free. A swooshing, spiraling descent drops you back into Ferndale, and leaves you finishing the ride with the perfect combination of feelings: accomplishment for riding 100 miles and exhilaration for getting to end them with a thrilling descent.

The Basics

Start: Intersection of Ocean St. and Main St. in downtown Ferndale.

Length: 100 miles.

Terrain: Three extended climbs, many rolling hills, heavy winds with gusts of sand on coast. Temperatures can vary dramatically, so dress in layers.

Food: You can get a good breakfast in Ferndale, right on Main Street. There's a store in Honeydew where you can buy some snacks for lunch and stock up on food to carry you through the day. Back in Ferndale, treat yourself to a heaping big meal.

For more information: RSVP, P.O. Box 275, Eureka, CA 95502; (800) 995–VELO.

Miles & Directions

- 0.0 South on Ocean St. at the intersection of Ocean and Main.
- 3.7 Straight past Waddington Rd.; Ocean St. becomes Grizzly Bluff Rd.
- 5.4 Pass Grizzly Bluff School.
- 13.1 Grizzly Bluff Rd. becomes Blue Slide Rd.; descend into Rio Dell. Right onto Wildwood Ave.
- 14.4 Scotia. Pass Pacific Lumber Mill.
- 15.9 Enter Hwy. 101S. Yes, this is a legal bike route!
- 21.7 Exit Hwy. 101 at Pepperwood. Left at stop sign onto Avenue of the Giants.
- 31.7 Right onto Bull Creek Rd./Honeydew exit under 101.
- 38.0 Albee Creek.
- 46.7 Begin ascent of Panther Gap.

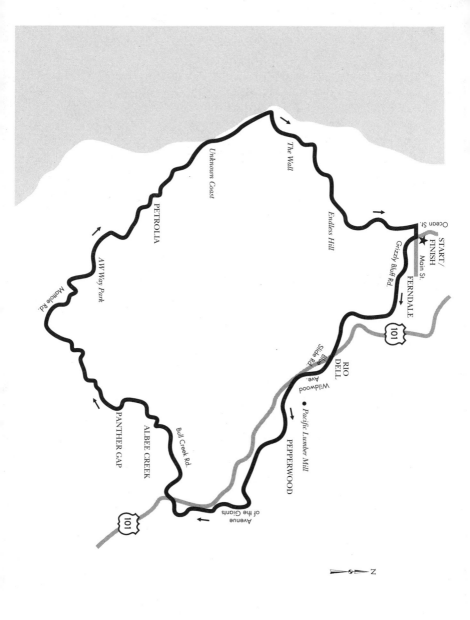

START/
FINISH

FERNDALE

Ocean St.

Main St.

Grizzly Bluff Rd.

The Wall

Endless Hill

Unknown Coast

PETROLIA

A W Way Park

Mattole Rd.

PANTHER GAP

ALBEE CREEK

Bull Creek Rd.

Avenue of the Giants

PEPPERWOOD

Pacific Lumber Mill

Wildwood Ave.

Blue Slide Rd.

RIO DELL

101

101

N

- 48.3 Summit.
- 63.0 AW Way Park.
- 69.0 Petrolia. Stay on paved road through town.
- 73.0 Unknown Coast.
- 81.5 Begin ascent of The Wall; 18 percent grade.
- 82.5 Summit.
- 86.7 Begin climb of The Endless Hill.
- 96.0 Summit.
- 100.0 Sharp right at bottom of Wildcat Grade. Ride ends at Ocean and Main in Ferndale.

2

Dyerville Loop Challenge

*Humboldt Redwoods State Park—Founders' Grove—
Dyerville Loop Road—Humboldt Redwoods
State Park—Avenue of the Giants—Myers Flat—
Weott—Founders' Grove*

> *Is it anaerobic agony or endorphin ecstasy? Sheer lunacy or
> athletic artistry?*
>   —Barbara Hanscome, *California Bicyclist*

It is said that the legendary Bigfoot, monstrous icon of the far-out 1970s, has been routinely spotted in the wilds of Humboldt County and the Humboldt Redwoods State Park. And on your bike, alone, in the solitude of an untamed forest, it's easy to shelve your jaded 1990s sensibility and embrace a world where fairies, gnomes, and even Bigfoot roam freely, ready to pop out from around the next corner.

There are times on the Dyerville Loop Challenge that anything seems possible. In between the few clusters of homes that could loosely be called towns, the ride is eerily quiet. In wet, deep green forests, ancestral redwoods stand stoic and unyielding: thousands of stories to tell, thousands of secrets kept. Out of the woodlands the Eel River snakes gently through open pasturelands where skinny-armed trees wave psychedelically from shimmery green branches. Roads climb abruptly to nowhere, only to drop back down again. And on this ride life presents itself as creepily mystical, uncanny, fantastic.

Although this loop ride is only 23 miles, there are many reasons to deem it a challenge. You'll immediately leave the flat, cool forest of Humboldt Redwoods State Park for the warmer, open fields of the surrounding area, so dress in layers; you won't want that long-sleeved jersey for more than a few miles. The roads are steep and rough for the first 9 miles, and the steepest and longest of the many climbs charges up a dirt and gravel fire road. With its steep switchbacks and numerous false summits, this unrelenting road does its best to defeat even the most intrepid of road bikers. To make it easier try wider tires if your bike will allow for them. Or bring a mountain bike or hybrid; the ride is short enough that it can be done comfortably on just about any bike as long as it has a wide gear ratio.

As you near the summit of this grand climb, the grade mellows out a bit, and with your nose out of the proverbial grindstone, you're free to look up, wipe the sweat from your brow, and see where your legs have taken you. Beyond the dense trees that form a cool canopy above, you'll see glimpses of far-off snow-covered peaks, as well as the Eel River, tiny now and far below.

High above the tall redwoods and state park tourists, this virtually carless road summits at a small community of modest homes, many of which are little more than dilapidated shacks with washing machines and the like piled up on sagging porches. There are no stores. No gas stations. No schools. Just small farms and clusters of country mailboxes with Dyerville Loop Road addresses.

You are in the middle of nowhere, yet only 5 miles away from the security of organized nature at Humboldt Redwoods State Park and the famed Avenue of the Giants. As you drop down Eel Creek Road back to the park, notice the dramatic terrain change from rolling, hilltop pastures to the lush valley of the redwood groves.

The flat terrain of the Avenue of the Giants is a gorgeous reprieve from the steep grades of Dyerville Loop and Eel River roads. The cool damp air massages your burning quads, and on the Avenue of the Giants, you're back to being a tourist again, leaving the rugged-adventurer stuff far behind on that gnarly dirt road. This comfort, however, brings a compromise: The Avenue of the Giants can be rather trafficky, making it best to plan your ride in the spring or fall, before the droves of Winnebagos descend.

On your bike, it's easy to make impromptu stops on the Avenue of the Giants to enjoy the dank, dark redwood groves. You also can drop in on the small but impressive visitor center, check out the eccentric locals in Myers Flat, stop in Weott for snacks, or just head back to the ride's start and finish at Founders' Grove. Here you can peel off your biking shoes, don your hiking boots, and take a short and easy hike on the Founders' Grove nature trail to stretch out your legs and soak up the wonder of the natural world.

The Basics

Start: Founders' Grove, on the Avenue of the Giants, in Humboldt Redwoods State Park.
Length: 23 miles.
Terrain: Steep, extended climbing. Rough roads; 2.2 miles of climbing on dirt and gravel road. Little to no traffic on Dyerville Loop Rd. and Elk Creek Rd. Weekend and tourist traffic on Avenue of the Giants.
Food: Two diners are located in Myers Flat, and there's a store with fresh fruit and snacks in Weott.
For more information: Humboldt Redwoods State Park, P.O. Box 100, Weott, CA 95571; (707) 946–2409.

Miles & Directions

- 0.0 Right onto Dyerville Loop Rd. from Founders' Grove parking lot.
- 0.5 Leave Humboldt Redwoods State Park.
- 0.6 Begin climb.
- 1.5 Summit.
- 2.2 Ride under subway; pass Redwood Area Seventh-Day Adventist Church.
- 3.7 Cross railroad track; begin climb.
- 4.7 Summit.
- 6.5 Dyerville Loop Rd. intersects with McCann Rd.; continue straight on Dyerville Loop Rd.

DYERVILLE

START/FINISH
Redwood Area
Seventh-Day
Adventist Church

WEOTT

Humboldt
Redwoods
State Park

Visitor
Center

Avenue of the Giants

FOUNDERS' GROVE

Avenue of the Giants

MYERS FLAT

Avenue of the Giants

Dyerville Loop Rd.

McCANN

McCann Rd.

Elk Creek Rd.

Dyerville Loop Rd.

Dyerville Loop Rd.

Sequoia (Whitlow) Rd.

N

- 6.7 Cross railroad track. Dyerville Loop Rd. turns to dirt. Begin steep climb.
- 8.9 Summit at Sequoia (Whitlow) Rd. Continue straight on Dyerville Loop Rd.
- 10.0 Right onto Elk Creek Rd. Follow sign that says HWY. 101 5 MILES.
- 12.8 Right onto Avenue of the Giants at the stop sign.
- 14.6 Myers Flat. Ride under 101N.
- 18.8 Humboldt Redwoods State Park visitor center.
- 20.4 Weott.
- 20.7 Hike & Bike Camp.
- 22.8 Right at Founders' Grove.
- 23.0 Ride ends at Founders' Grove parking lot.

3

Comptche Cruise

Mendocino—Little River—Van Damme State Park
Pygmy Forest—Comptche—Mendocino

> *I shall be telling this with a sigh/Somewhere ages and ages*
> *hence:/Two roads diverged in a wood, and I—/I took the one*
> *less traveled by,/And that has made all the difference.*
> —Robert Frost, "The Road Not Taken"

Highway 1 curls groggily into the misty oceanside town of Mendocino. From the distance the town looks tiny and sleepy as it lunges forth from the highway, jutting out on a rocky, jagged edge to meet the Pacific Ocean. A closer inspection, however, reveals a lot of tourist-driven cheesiness behind the town's charming New England facade. Yet despite its unabashed commercialism, Mendocino *is*—dare I say it?—cute. But where do you draw the line between cuteness and gaudiness? How long can you shop? How many driftwood clocks and paintings of whales can you look at?

This, of course, is why you have a bike. The magic of Mendocino lies outside its city limits and simply cannot be properly appreciated or explored within the confines of an automobile. From its rocky coast to its densely forested inland mountains, Mendocino County is perhaps the most dramatically beautiful county in all of California. And the quiet country roads leading to middle-of-nowhere towns provide a brief glimpse into the lives of random town residents from all kinds of backgrounds. Stop for a minute and listen to their stories: They'll happily tell you how they count their blessings daily for being fortunate enough to have all this unadulterated peacefulness right in their backyards.

The Comptche Cruise begins by exiting historic (hysteric?) downtown Mendocino and heading south on the twisty, turny, drop-off-the-face-of-the-earth Highway 1. After 3 miles of riding past oceanside resorts and B&Bs, you'll hit the unassuming Little River Road. This is the kind of road that immediately makes your lips curl upward, because you know, just by looking at the arching trees above it and the way it rambles off to nowhere special, that you've found a killer backroad, the kind of road that cyclists love and car drivers hate.

After less than 3 miles on Little River Road, you'll come to the Van Damme State Park Pygmy Forest—a place that lives up to its intriguing name and is well worth a quick look. A raised wooden walkway twists and turns in a maniacal maze through decades-old trees that stand no taller than 4 feet because of the highly acidic soil content and poor drainage.

At the end of Little River Road, you reach the beginning of Comptche-Ukiah Road. There's no sign to tell you what road you're on or where it leads to, but turn right and you'll be heading for Comptche, which is another 9 miles of near-orgasmic cycling away. The Comptche-Ukiah Road is cut into the side of a mountain with a severe dropoff to the redwood valleys far below it. To the left your backdrop is an unending horizon of tree-covered mountains, dreamily softened by the fog that often hovers at their tops. To the right a lush wall of damp, thick forest hugs the side of the road.

After you have cycled only a few miles on this glorious road's summit, the road swoops downward to Comptche. Four miles of descending carries you out of the forested woodlands and into the open grasslands, complete with small farms and houses, lazy cows and sheep. From here it's 5 relatively flat miles to the booming metropolis of Comptche, featuring one post office, one store with gas station, one church, and one school. Stop for a snack at the market and relax with the Comptche locals, who can often be found hanging out on the one bench in front of the one store.

This is a turnaround point, so fuel up for the extended climb back on Comptche-Ukiah Road. This long, gradual ascent provides the same forested vistas but from an opposite—and much slower— perspective. When you get to Little River Road, continue straight

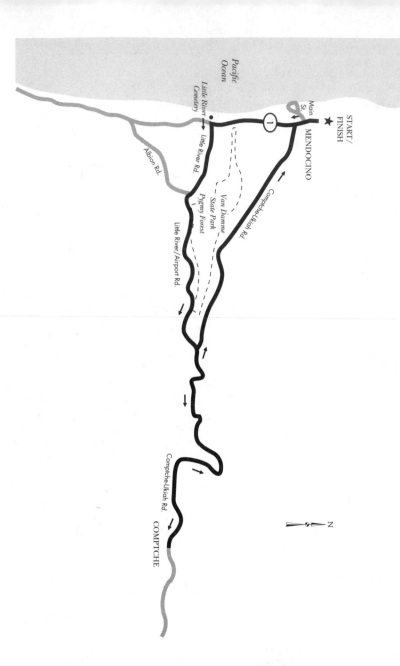

on Comptche-Ukiah for a fast and easy descent offering awe-inspiring views of the Pacific Ocean and Mendocino. It's a great payback for all the climbing and a perfect way to end a ride.

Back on Highway 1, you're less than 1 mile away from Mendocino. And after a hearty day of backroads cycling, it's easier to justify one's inherent American urge to indulge in the consumer orgy—so get off your bike, visit town, and eat, drink, and shop to your heart's content.

The Basics

Start: Mendocino, at the intersection of Main St. and Hwy. 1.
Length: 32.9 miles.
Terrain: One major climb, some rollers, lengthy flat stretches on quiet backroads.
Food: Health food markets and all sorts of restaurants in Mendocino; one small store in Comptche.
For more information: Catch a Canoe & Bicycles, Too! at The Stanford Inn by the Sea, Hwy. 1 at Comptche-Ukiah Rd., Mendocino; (707) 937–0273.

Miles & Directions

- 0.0 Right onto Hwy. 1 at the intersection of Hwy. 1 and Main St. in Mendocino.
- 3.1 Left onto Little River/Airport Rd., immediately past Little River Cemetery.
- 5.8 Van Damme State Park Pygmy Forest to the left, Albion Rd. to the right. Continue straight on Little River Rd.
- 9.0 Little River Rd. Ts at an unmarked road, which is Comptche-Ukiah Rd. Turn right.
- 18.0 Comptche. Turnaround point.
- 26.1 Intersect with Little River Rd.; continue straight on Comptche-Ukiah Rd.
- 32.3 Comptche-Ukiah Rd. Ts at Hwy. 1. Turn right.
- 32.9 Ride ends at intersection of Hwy. 1 and Main St. in Mendocino.

4

Patrick's Point Cruise

Arcata—Clam Beach State Park—Trinidad—
Patrick's Point—Arcata

If you give it an inch—Nay, a hair—It will take a yard—
Nay, an evolution—And give you a contusion, or, like
enough, a perforated kneecap.
—Francis E. Willard, *How I Learned to Ride the Bicycle*

On a misty gray day in the North Coast town of Arcata, when the chill seeps right through to your bones, straddling a cold metal bike is just about as appealing as skinny-dipping in the Arctic Circle. Even in the summer, frigid fog can hang over the coast for most of the morning, creating an overcast mood that leads to lingering over coffee, reading the paper in pajamas, analyzing cloud formations for signs of rain—anything but suiting up in Lycra and slinging your leg over a top tube.

Problem is, waiting for sunshine often means sacrificing a good part of your day. So cyclists in Arcata have learned to adapt. You'll see them out there—rain or shine—with fenders on their bikes, waterproof windbreakers on their backs, and layers of bike clothing ready to be peeled off at the first sight of sunshine. And if you're able to muster up enough internal willpower to get out there and join them, you'll realize they aren't just enduring the weather—they're actually enjoying it.

The Patrick's Point Cruise is a favorite local out-and-back that provides dramatic views of the jagged North Coast, including 3 miles of windswept coastal riding on a stretch of road that seems poised on the edge of the earth and ready to crumble into the Pacific Ocean at any moment.

The ride starts at the Life Cycle bike shop in downtown Arcata, a gently accepting type of town where the macrobiotic-diet crowd (intelligentsia from Humboldt State University) mixes easily with the meat-and-potatoes crowd (farming and lumber-industry families who've lived there all their lives). Two miles out of Arcata, the flat and fast roads become increasingly rural; houses are separated by large plots of farmland where cows graze loosely in wide-open fields. The voluptuous curves of Mad River Road eventually lead to the river, where an arched bike and pedestrian bridge links recreation seekers to the Hammond Bike Path. A well-traveled throughway, this route connects Mad River Park with Hiller Park and, eventually, the ocean.

The bike path ends 0.5 mile from Highway 101N, which is perfectly legal for bikes and only moderately trafficky (as well as being the only road north). You can, however, avoid a good deal of it by exiting at Clam Beach State Park, where you can ride alongside sandy dunes instead of smoggy cars. At the end of the park road, you'll have approximately 1.5 miles of highway to endure, including crossing a short bridge with no shoulder and hauling yourself up the ride's only extended climb (less than 0.5 mile) to the Westhaven Drive exit.

From here the slight Scenic Drive winds bold and treacherous above the Pacific, clinging to the edge of a rocky cliff for dear life. For motorists it may be a white-knuckle drive, but for cyclists it's nothing short of cathartic. Below the road, waves roll in to massage the craggy sand. In the distance Patrick's Point juts abruptly out from land toward ocean, standing triumphantly and defiantly above the waves that crash around it.

A rolling 5 miles on Patrick's Point Road, thick with trees and intermittent coastal views, brings you to the entrance of Patrick's Point State Park. But it's 1 mile farther to the *actual* Patrick's Point, which stands more than 200 feet above the ocean and provides unsurpassed views of the rocky, misty, stoically beautiful North Coast. Excursions to Patrick's Point, which is often much colder than the rest of the park due to bitter winds, usually require putting on that windbreaker you've had stuffed in your jersey pocket for the last 15 miles.

If you're finding it hard to tear yourself away, the cold air may serve as the final catalyst to get you back on your bike. From the park just reverse directions and head back in the opposite way toward Arcata. If you're burned out on riding, there's even a bus that heads back to Arcata at the entrance to 101S—and it lets bikes on board. But perhaps a better way to get yourself through the ride if you're feeling weary is to try visualization: Think beer. When the ride ends in Arcata, you'll be less than 0.5 mile from the center of town, where a hearty microbrewed beer awaits at the award-winning Humboldt Brewery.

The Basics

Start: Life Cycle bike shop at 16th St. and G St. in downtown Arcata.
Length: 46 miles.
Terrain: Mostly flat, with a few rolling hills and one extended climb; 4 miles of moderately trafficked highway riding.
Food: Best bet for food is Arcata. Lots of healthy snacks that you can pack in your jersey for the ride. Energy bars at Life Cycle bike shop. There's a small store 6 miles into the ride at the intersection of School Rd. Also, you can purchase picnic foods and deli sandwiches at the large grocery store in Trinidad, just 5 miles from Patrick's Point, where Scenic Rd. becomes Patrick's Point Rd.
For more information: Life Cycle bike shop, 1593 G St., Arcata, CA 95521; (707) 822–7755.

Miles & Directions

- 0.0 Left onto 16th at 16th St. and G St.
- 0.3 Left onto L.
- 0.4 Right onto 15th, then right onto Alliance.
- 1.5 Left onto Spear Ave.

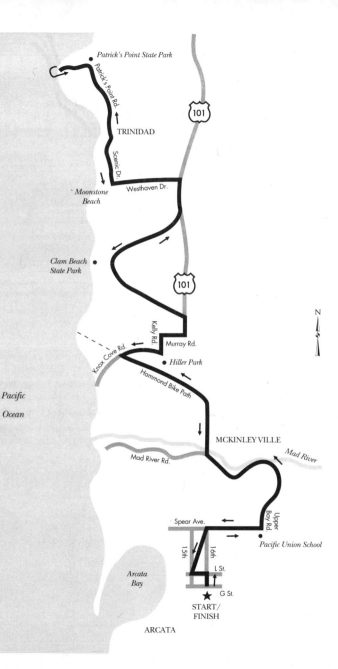

Patrick's Point State Park

Patrick's Point Rd.

101

TRINIDAD

Scenic Dr.

Westhaven Dr.

Moonstone
Beach

Clam Beach
State Park

101

Kelly Rd.

Murray Rd.

Knox Cove Rd.

Hiller Park

Hammond Bike Path

Pacific

Ocean

MCKINLEYVILLE

Mad River

Mad River Rd.

N

Spear Ave.

Upper
Bay Rd.

15th

16th

Pacific Union School

Arcata
Bay

L St.

G St.

★
START/
FINISH

ARCATA

- 2.1 Left onto Upper Bay Rd. across from Pacific Union School.
- 2.8 Right onto Mad River Rd.
- 5.3 Right onto bike/pedestrian bridge marked HAMMOND TRAIL/COASTAL TRAIL.
- 6.4 Veer onto Hammond Bike Path.
- 6.6 Continue on bike path into Hiller Park.
- 7.4 Pacific Ocean. Right onto Knox Cove Rd.
- 7.5 Left onto Kelly Rd.
- 7.6 Right at road's end onto Murray Rd.
- 8.0 Left onto 101N toward Crescent City.
- 10.4 Exit 101N at Clam Beach State Park.
- 10.6 Left of Clam Beach.
- 12.1 Cross 101 overpass. Left on 101N.
- 12.6 **Caution!** Cross short bridge on 101 with no shoulder.
- 12.9 Begin climb.
- 13.3 Summit at Westhaven Dr.; exit at Westhaven Dr.
- 13.5 Left to Moonstone Beach, then right onto Scenic Dr.
- 16.8 Trinidad. Scenic Dr. becomes Patrick's Point Rd.
- 22.1 Left into Patrick's Point State Park.
- 23.0 Patrick's Point. Turnaround point.

* Return following the same route, with two notes: Exit 101S at Little River Beach (by the weigh station) for the Clam Beach stretch that temporarily gets you off the highway. Get off 101 for good at the Murray Rd. exit. You'll reach a sign that says NOT A THROUGH ROAD, but continue on—it does take you to the Hammond Bike Path.

5

Trinity Alps Challenge

Weaverville—Whiskeytown-Shasta-Trinity National Recreation Area—Trinity Lake— Lewiston—Weaverville

> *Never measure the height of a mountain until you have reached the top. Then you will see how low it was.*
> —Dag Hammarskjöld, former UN secretary-general, *Markings*

Tucked into the folds of Highway 299's mountainous undulations, the town of Weaverville stands as a slight bit of civilization encircled by Trinity County's 3,220 square miles of rushing rivers, snowy peaks, expansive lakes, and protected wilderness areas. Relatively unchanged from its historic mining days, the town features wooden sidewalks and balconies that give it an Old West feel; one look around town and you can't help but ponder the rough-and-tumble lives of California's first settlers.

But get on your bike and pedal just a few miles away from this sleepy hamlet and another history unfolds. The Trinity Alps mountains—ancestral predecessors to Weaverville, mining, and humankind—have their own stories to tell. And grinding up the side of one of their ridges on your bike is just the way to listen to what these mountains have to say.

The Trinity Alps Challenge immediately departs town and heads for Shasta-Trinity State Park and the Whiskeytown-Shasta-Trinity National Recreation Area, where one climb leads to another climb leads to another climb until you are high above sprawling Trinity

Lake and dizzy with adrenaline. From the summit of Trinity Dam Boulevard, white jagged peaks cradle the tiny mountaintop road with all the power and precariousness of an unpredictable giant.

Here all your climbing pays off in the form of a long, steep descent. As you drop down to Trinity Lake, you'll have less of an opportunity to enjoy the natural beauty of your surroundings but more of a chance to revel in the pure thrill of plummeting down a fast mountain road. At the bottom of the descent, you get a bit of a reprieve from all the previous ups and downs as you ride along the base of the lake, where campgrounds, boat launches, and fishing camps dot your path.

A 1-mile climb out of the Whiskeytown-Shasta-Trinity Recreation Area marks the outskirts of Lewiston. Another historic mining town, this curious little settlement crops up spontaneously and is just as quickly engulfed by wilderness. The small town forms a tiny sanctuary from the forested wilds of the Trinity Alps and consists of an original Old West hotel, a few antiques shops, a B&B, and little else.

From Lewiston the ride back to Weaverville follows Rush Creek Road, a lightly traveled route with sporadic country homes hidden behind walls of trees. There's one more extended climb that lasts for only 1 mile but seems endless—perhaps because you're almost home, perhaps because you've been climbing all day. After reaching the top, pedal 7 more miles and you're back to Highway 3, which features a long, luscious descent back into Weaverville.

From here you can look back at the Trinity Alps looming impossibly high in the distance and think about how far you've gone, about all the miles of climbing you've hammered into your muscles. From Weaverville's valley the distant mountains looks murderous, hardcore. But in the afterglow of the ride, all pain is forgotten and anything seems possible. Tuck that feeling away in some corner of your mind and don't let go of it. A time will inevitably come when you'll need to rely on the glory of the past to pull you through the pain of the present. Because there will always be another challenge. There will always be a higher mountain to climb.

The Basics

Start: Intersection of Hwy. 299 and Hwy. 3 in downtown Weaverville.

Length: 44.8 miles.

Terrain: Mountain roads, many extended climbs, few flat sections; narrow roads with little traffic.

Food: There's a good health food store right on Main Street in Weaverville where you can stock up on food for the ride. Upon departing Weaverville, you'll find no opportunities for food until Lewiston (mile 28), which has a very limited selection. Back in Weaverville there are plenty of postride restaurants.

For more information: The owner of the Old Lewiston Inn has mapped out bike routes in the area for his B&B guests. Contact Connor Nixon, Deadwood Rd. Historic Area, P.O. Box 688, Lewiston, CA 96052; (916) 778–3385. Trinity County Chamber of Commerce may also be able to help, but most people in the area seem to be mountain bikers. Bring your mountain bike, too, if you can. There are endless miles of fire roads and single-track trails. Trinity County Chamber of Commerce, 317 Main St., Weaverville, CA 96093; (916) 623–6101.

Miles & Directions

- 0.0 Take Hwy. 3 toward Trinity Lakes from Main St. (Hwy. 299) in downtown Weaverville; begin climbing out of town.
- 2.8 Summit.
- 4.2 Enter Shasta-Trinity State Park.
- 8.1 Right onto Trinity Dam Blvd.; begin climbing.
- 10.5 Summit at intersection of Haylock Ridge (to the left) and Buckeye Ridge (to the right). Continue straight.
- 12.9 Enter Whiskeytown-Shasta-Trinity National Recreation Area.
- 13.4 Begin climbing again!
- 14.7 Summit.

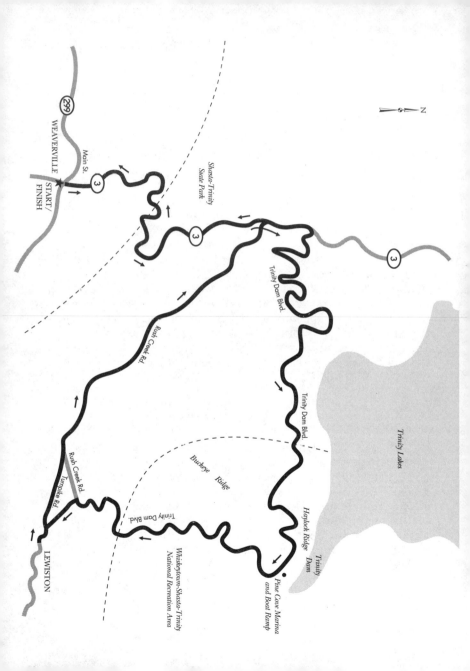

- 16.7 Trinity Vista Overlook; begin descent.
- 19.2 Trinity Dam Vista.
- 22.9 Pass Pine Cove Marina and Boat Ramp.
- 25.0 Copper Gulch Campground; begin another climb.
- 25.9 Summit.
- 27.2 Leave Whiskeytown-Shasta-Trinity National Recreation Area.
- 27.8 Straight past Rush Creek Rd. and the sign TO WEAVERVILLE.
- 27.9 Right onto Deadwood Rd.
- 28.0 Lewiston.
- 28.8 Right onto Turnpike Rd. over old bridge.
- 29.0 Left onto Rush Creek Rd.; begin climbing.
- 30.0 Summit.
- 37.6 Left onto Hwy. 3 to Weaverville.
- 43.4 Weaverville city limits.
- 44.8 Ride ends at Main St. in Weaverville.

San Francisco Bay Area

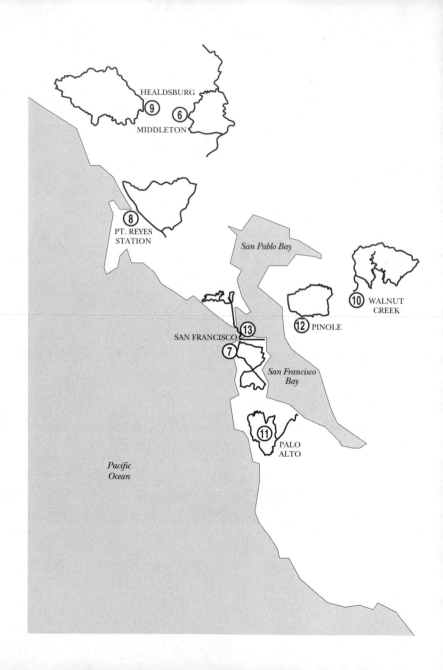

HEALDSBURG

⑨ ⑥

MIDDLETON

⑧

PT. REYES
STATION

San Pablo Bay

⑩ WALNUT
CREEK

⑬

SAN FRANCISCO

⑫ PINOLE

⑦

*San Francisco
Bay*

⑪ PALO
ALTO

*Pacific
Ocean*

San Francisco Bay Area

6. Harbin Hot Springs Challenge 38
7. San Francisco to Mt. San Bruno Urban Cruise 43
8. Cheese Company Cruise 49
9. Skaggs Spring Classic 53
10. Around and over Diablo Classic 59
11. Sky Londa Cruise 64
12. Pinole Ramble 68
13. Headlands Loop Cruise 73

6

Harbin Hot Springs Challenge

*Harbin Hot Springs—Middleton—Petrified Forest—
Calistoga—Harbin Hot Springs*

> *Riding a bike with no shirt on is very fun. Especially in the rain. Makes you ride faster, too.*
>
> —Greta Snyder, *Mudflap*

If you've ever felt weighed down by the clothes on your back, it's time to shed all superfluous coverings and head for Harbin Hot Springs, a clothing-optional, 1,200-acre resort resting sedately in the hills of California's Lake County, just two hours northeast of San Francisco. No California experience is truly complete without a trip to Harbin, which is run by the Heart Consciousness Church, a New Age group advocating holistic health and spiritual renewal. And no bike book is complete without a tour of the area's surrounding backroads, which have the power to bring even the most ardent heathens closer to God. This land is nothing short of divine.

To understand how cool the Harbin Hot Springs resort is, try the following exercise. Dream up your perfect day of cycling and then compare it with this:

A warm day of riding on secluded roads. Nary a car nor a cyclist in sight. Killer climbs and unsurpassed hilltop views. Untraveled pavement spiraling endlessly downward. Weary limbs and endorphin highs at ride's end. And then: soft, natural spring pools of varying temperatures to soak in. A sauna. A masseuse. Sunbathing on redwood decks. A huge vegetarian meal prepared for you. A free movie. A night of peaceful sleep among the redwoods—beside a babbling brook or in a cozy cabin.

This is not a dream. You have not gone to biker heaven; you've gone to Harbin. The Harbin Hot Springs Challenge is not just a ride. And you don't do it in one day. It's more like a life experience—with some awesome cycling thrown in to make it all the better. The good folks at Harbin have made camping easy and desirable with gorgeous wooded surroundings and redwood decks built especially for pitching your tent. (Should you have to get dirty when you camp? Perish the thought!) So make a weekend out of this ride—or longer, if you can manage it.

While topless or naked cycling certainly wouldn't turn many heads on Harbin's property, clothing is highly recommended for the outlying country roads that this ride traverses. Also recommended is a road bike with wide, durable tires—such as Continental touring tires—or a mountain bike or good hybrid. The 3-mile climb up Western Mine Road turns from pavement to dirt fire road after the first mile. This is the only dirt road on the entire ride, but the bumpy road does demand some attention to equipment. There's also a greater potential for flatting, so make doubly sure you've got a spare tube as well as a patch kit.

The steep and tiring Western Mine climb begins after only 6.7 miles of cycling. The road turns to dirt at mile 7.7 and becomes paved again at the summit (mile 9.9). After all the jostling and sweating to get to the top, the smooth, picturesque, and never-ending descent can only be described as godlike. For the next 20 miles, the route is completely and utterly rural. You'll pass few homes and even fewer cars on the ride. And if you do feel the urge to ride naked, these nearly deserted roads are probably the best upon which to do it.

Cyclists continue to be treated to this noble countryside until they reach Petrified Forest Road, which involves a more trafficky climb and finally leads to the Petrified Forest at mile 30.5. Get off your bike and take a look around. After you've had your fill, it's back to Petrified Forest Road for 4 miles until hitting Highway 128 and, 1 mile later, the less crowded Highway 29.

The ride gets even more touristy here as you cycle into Calistoga, land of commercialized hot springs and spas. Land of restaurants and amenities and cute shops. It's a great place to stop, but after a hard day of riding, you'll be glad you're staying on Harbin's tranquil, laid-back land. Visit ye olde ice cream shoppes and the like in Calistoga; then it's a straight shot on Highway 29 back to Middleton. From there you're 5 miles away from a luxurious soak and a huge, holistic feast at Harbin.

The Basics

Start: Harbin Hot Springs campground. From U.S. 101 in Geyserville, take Rte. 128 east to Calistoga, then Rte. 29 north to Middleton. Turn left at the stoplight, then right at Barnes St. Four miles to Harbin Springs Rd., which leads to Harbin Hot Springs.
Length: 57.9 miles.
Terrain: Extended climbing and lengthy descents. Some rough roads, including 1 mile of dirt fire road. Mostly rural roads, with a few high-traffic areas.
Food: There's a very limited general store on Harbin's property, mainly carrying all-natural snacks. An all-purpose convenience store is located in Middleton, 4.2 miles from the ride's start. No more food options until Calistoga, at 35.3 miles.
For more information: Harbin Hot Springs, P.O. Box 782, Middletown, CA 95461; (707) 987–2477.

Miles & Directions

- ■ 0.0 Harbin Hot Springs camping area, Harbin Springs Rd.
- ■ 2.8 Veer right onto Big Canyon Rd. Big Canyon becomes Barnes Rd.
- ■ 4.2 Left onto Main St. into Middleton.
- ■ 4.4 Right onto Rte. 29.
- ■ 6.7 Right onto Western Mine Rd.
- ■ 7.7 Road turns to dirt.

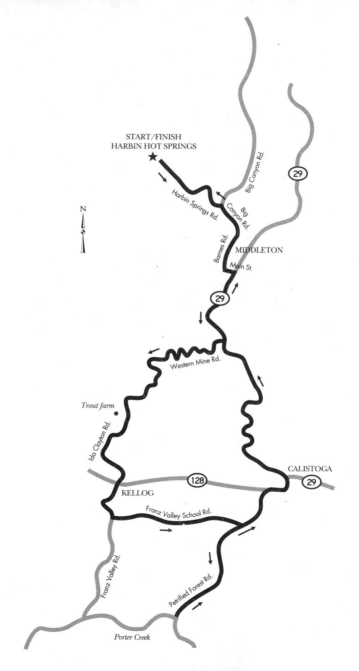

START/FINISH
HARBIN HOT SPRINGS

N

MIDDLETON

Harbin Springs Rd.

Big Canyon Rd.

Big Canyon Rd.

Barnes Rd.

Main St.

29

29

Western Mine Rd.

Trout farm

Ida Clayton Rd.

CALISTOGA

128

KELLOG

29

Franz Valley School Rd.

Franz Valley Rd.

Petrified Forest Rd.

Porter Creek

- ■ 9.9 Summit. Road becomes Ida Clayton Rd. and turns back to pavement. **Caution!** Steep, winding descent on one-lane road.
- ■ 10.9 Trout farm.
- ■ 18.1 Left on Rte. 29 (unmarked).
- ■ 18.3 Right onto Franz Valley Rd.
- ■ 19.2 Stay to the right and continue on Franz Valley Rd.
- ■ 22.8 Left onto Franz Valley School Rd.
- ■ 25.4 Enter Napa County.
- ■ 27.3 Road ends at Petrified Forest Rd.; turn right.
- ■ 30.5 Petrified Forest, turnaround point. Turn left back onto Petrified Forest Rd.
- ■ 34.4 Right onto Rte. 128.
- ■ 35.3 Left onto Rte. 29 into Calistoga.
- ■ 52.3 Left onto Main St. in Middleton.
- ■ 52.5 Right onto Barnes St.
- ■ 55.1 Left onto Harbin Springs Rd.
- ■ 57.9 Ride ends at Harbin Hot Springs camping area.

7

San Francisco to Mt. San Bruno Urban Cruise

Golden Gate Park—Great Highway—the Sunset—
Daly City—Mt. San Bruno State Park—the Mission—
the Castro—Golden Gate Park

> Forget the damned motor car and build the cities for lovers
> and friends.
>
> —Lewis Mumford, *My Work and Days*

There are cyclists out there who spend their entire lives seeking nirvana in the ultimate backroad. Tirelessly, doggedly, idealistically, they search for that transcendent stretch of tarmac that will elevate their cycling from a recreational outlet to a spiritual experience.

If you've been riding long enough, you've no doubt felt that place where body, soul, and bicycle come together for a brief moment of unworldly ecstasy. And it sends you. And you want more. A more beautiful road. A higher peak. A more peaceful portion of pavement.

Funny thing is, the path to enlightenment is quite often the obvious path, the one that's been there all along. Such is the joy of the urban ride: the blurred colors and smells of city life, the cacophony of the street sounds buzzing in your ears, the self-sufficiency of using your bike for transportation and exploration—not just for recreation.

This is the beauty of the San Francisco to Mt. San Bruno Urban Cruise. The subtleties of San Francisco living, of the reality of urban existence, are what this ride is all about. The ride starts in Golden Gate Park. As you begin your trek at the brilliant green lawn of the bright white, fairy-tale-like building that houses the plant conservatory, the muted colors of the city are washed away and replaced by blue skies, green grass, and pink tulips.

But this brilliant departure from reality is short-lived. After 5 miles of riding, the relative peace of the park and the paradisiacal ocean views from the Great Highway are replaced by car doors flinging open, booming bass droning from stereos, and the pungent emissions of stagnant garbage, heavy exhaust, and roasted coffee. Tiny neighborhoods and microcosmic communities dot your path as you head up Mission Street toward the outskirts of town, with Mt. San Bruno drawing nearer—and your impending climb seeming all the bigger.

The mountain trudge begins at mile 13.5 and doesn't let up until you summit Mt. San Bruno at mile 16.7. *California Bicyclist's* former Associate Editor Barbara Hanscome describes the climb, which is the site of a traditional New Year's Day hillclimb race, as "guaranteeing anaerobic agony for any cyclist who dares to climb it."

Whatever agony you may experience, the view from the top is well worth flexing your quads over. If it's not storming, freezing, or blowing you over up there, stop long enough to check out the view. Turn one way and you'll see downtown San Francisco, the Bay Bridge, and the East Bay stretching out into the distance. Walk to the other side and survey the Peninsula's sprawling suburbs, the majestic Golden Gate Bridge, and the distant Pacific Ocean. From your peaceful mountaintop vista, the urban sprawl that you and your bike were recently battling seems sedated and calmed—almost still. The chaos of a million personal dramas are being played out below you, yet for this one moment everything is serene, virtually soundless except for the whipping wind.

Get the most out of your descent as you snake back into the city, because the return route includes one more steep, punchy climb at mile 25, as you tackle an obligatory short but steep San Francisco hill on Dolores Street.

Your final 3 miles of riding traverse through two of San Francisco's most interesting neighborhoods: the Mission and the Castro. If you haven't spent much time in San Francisco, you'll definitely want some out-of-the-saddle exploring time in at least one of these areas. And if you've worked up an appetite, take a right onto Dolores into the heart of the Mission for a monster burrito like you won't find anywhere else.

From here it's an easy ride back to Golden Gate Park and the conservatory, where you can join other cyclists and random fun lovers sprawled out on the abnormally bright green lawn. You've earned a right to dwell in the denial of the park's man-made perfection for a while, because you've seen reality. And you know that, in its own way, it's even better.

The Basics

Start: Golden Gate Park Conservatory. Enter the park at Stanyan St., and the conservatory is the large white building about 0.3 mile in on the main road, John F. Kennedy Dr.
Length: 28.1 miles.
Terrain: Abrupt, short but steep hills in San Francisco. One major climb up Mt. San Bruno. Potholes, ever-changing road construction sites, and narrow streets in the city.
Food: No real restaurants or stores in the park. Visit nearby Haight Street for stores where you can stock up on ride food or grab a slice of pizza or a burrito. Better yet, take a quick detour into the Mission at Mission Dolores Park (mile 25.2) and visit La Cumbre (515 Valencia) or one of the many other *taquerias* for the best burritos the city has to offer.
For more information: San Francisco Convention and Visitors' Bureau, 201 3rd St., Suite 900, San Francisco, CA 94103; (415) 974–6900.

Miles & Directions

- 0.0   From Golden Gate Park Conservatory, turn right onto John F. Kennedy Dr.

- 2.0 Stay on the main road as you pass the unmarked road around the lake to your left.
- 2.1 Buffalo field.
- 2.7 Turn right, still on John F. Kennedy Dr.
- 3.1 Pacific Ocean! Turn left onto Great Highway.
- 5.6 Turn left onto Sloat Blvd.
- 5.7 San Francisco Zoo.
- 7.4 Turn right onto 19th Ave.
- 7.5 Turn left onto Ocean Ave.
- 9.1 Veer right. Ocean Ave. ends; Geneva begins.
- 9.3 Cross over Hwy. 280.
- 9.8 Turn right onto Mission St.
- 11.1 Turn right onto Flourney.
- 11.2 Turn left onto San Jose Ave. Becomes Mission again. Entering Daly City.
- 12.5 Turn left onto E. Market.
- 13.5 E. Market becomes Guadalupe Canyon Pkwy. Pass sign ENTERING MT. SAN BRUNO STATE PARK. Begin climb.
- 14.8 Turn left at Mt. San Bruno State Park entrance. Take immediate right past ranger station onto Summit Rd. (also known as Tower Rd. or Radio Rd., but don't worry about names—there's not even a sign for it).
- 15.0 Ride under overpass.
- 16.7 Summit at radio towers. Turnaround point.
- 18.3 Turn left at ranger station.
- 18.4 Turn left onto Guadalupe Canyon Pkwy.
- 19.6 Turn left onto Carter.
- 19.9 Cow Palace.
- 20.3 Turn left onto Geneva.
- 21.4 Turn right onto Mission St.
- 22.7 Ride over freeway overpass; stay on Mission St.
- 24.1 Turn left onto 26th St.
- 24.5 Turn right onto Dolores St.
- 25.2 Mission Dolores Park.
- 25.4 Turn left onto 18th St.
- 25.9 Turn right onto Castro St.
- 26.6 Castro St. becomes Divisadero.

- 26.8 Left onto Fell St.
- 27.1 Panhandle Park parallel to Fell St. Get on bike path to avoid dog-eat-dog traffic scene.
- 27.8 Panhandle ends. Enter Golden Gate Park.
- 28.1 Ride ends at conservatory.

8

Cheese Company Cruise

Marin French Cheese Company—Marshall—Point Reyes Station—Marin French Cheese Company

> *Savor the accidental, perfect beauty of life in whatever small portions are dished out to you. And never question why you ride. Question only why you don't ride more.*
> —Mike Ferrentino, *California Bicyclist*

You know you're a real bicyclist when you actually start liking the smell of cow dung. It happens on pastoral roads as you're cycling past dumb, lovable cows that stare you down with their deep black eyes. And you're riding. And the sky is blue and the grass is green and the gentle breeze carries with it the smell of—cow dung. And for the first time ever, you find the odor wonderful and you breathe it in deeply and you ride and you're oh-so-happy just to be alive.

The Cheese Company Cruise is the kind of ride that has this potential. If you've never loved cows or the smell of their relievings, take this ride and then see how you feel. Its idyllic setting is made all the more beautiful precisely because you smell cows and ride past big sturdy barns. And when you do, you can almost feel the dignity and understand the truth behind the simple, hardworking lifestyle of the farmers who live there.

The ride begins at the Marin French Cheese Company, located on the Point Reyes–Petaluma Road between Novato and Petaluma. This is a popular bike ride for local cyclists, and you'll probably run into some of them relaxing on the cheese company's lawn while they recover or take a break from riding.

With its luscious cheeses and meticulously manicured property, the Marin French Cheese Company is the most commercialized spot on the entire bike route. Once you step into your pedals and turn onto Hicks Valley Road, you roll into a different world.

The first 10 miles provide fast and easy riding on intensely rural roads. Your whirring wheels and rhythmic breathing are the only audible sounds, and as you settle into this trancelike quiet, it's almost impossible to believe that you're only 40 miles away from the urban sprawl of San Francisco and its surrounding areas.

After exactly 10 miles you reach what's known by cyclists as the Marshall Wall. This 2-mile climb is an unrelenting pull with at least two false summits that laugh in your face as they reveal yet another hill for your downtrodden legs to tackle. Still, the name is more intimidating than the actual climb. And once you get to the top, the views of Point Reyes and Tomales Bay are absolutely euphoric. Then again, maybe it's just those endorphins that're coursing through your body.

The backside of the Marshall Wall is much steeper and makes for a great descent that you'll be thankful not to have to return on. Down in the tiny town of Marshall, you'll find rickety oyster bars and a few random stores perched on the edge of Tomales Bay. Following the Shoreline Highway, you'll get a rollercoaster ride of whoop-di-do pavement that's often made easier by benevolent tailwinds. After nearly 7 miles of this fun, you'll experience a few longer climbs before dropping down into the tiny burg of Point Reyes Station, a holistic little town with lots of charm and plenty of healthy food—so fuel up for your home stretch back to the cheese company.

You get even more sweet cows, rural scenery, and peaceful country-road stuff on the way back. And, of course, as fate would have it, there's another major climb less than 4 miles from the end of the ride. This final push begins just past the Nicasio Reservoir and heads upward on a fairly busy road back to the cheese company, where you can chill out and mooch free samples of cheese. Proper etiquette dictates that you do eventually buy something, but don't feel shy about sampling the goods. Even in your sweaty, dirty bike clothes, sporting your freshly plastered helmet-head, you won't be shunned—this is biking territory, and the folks are used to our kind here.

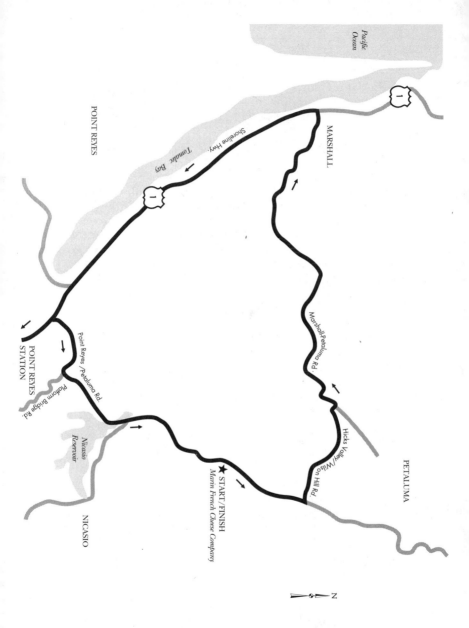

The Basics

Start: Marin French Cheese Company, Point Reyes–Petaluma Rd. Take Hwy. 101 to downtown Novato. From there take Novato Blvd. east until it intersects with Point Reyes–Petaluma Rd.
Length: 34.5 miles.
Terrain: Two major climbs; lots of rolling hills on smooth, quiet roads.
Food: The cheese company has—you guessed it—lots of cheese and cheese-related snacks, as well as chips, sodas, and delicious fruit. If you like raw oysters, stop in Marshall at one of the bayside oyster bars. Otherwise, you can stock up on snacks in Point Reyes Station. There's a great grocery store with a deli situated right on the main road.
For more information: Petaluma Area Chamber of Commerce, 215 Howard St., Petaluma, CA; (707) 762–2785.

Miles & Directions

- 0.0 From the cheese company, turn left onto Point Reyes–Petaluma Rd.
- 0.9 Left onto Hicks Valley/Wilson Hill Rd. to Marshall.
- 3.6 Left on Marshall–Petaluma Rd.
- 10.0 S/2 Aberdeen Angus Cattle Ranch. Begin climb up Marshall Wall!
- 12.0 Summit.
- 14.6 Marshall. Left onto Shoreline Hwy.
- 23.7 Veer right, staying on Hwy. 1 (formerly Shoreline Hwy.) into Point Reyes Station.
- 24.0 Point Reyes Station. Turnaround point. After sightseeing, ride back up the hill on Hwy. 1.
- 24.2 Veer right onto Point Reyes–Petaluma Rd.
- 28.1 Left at T intersection onto Platform Bridge Rd.
- 28.9 Nicasio Reservoir.
- 31.1 Begin climb.
- 32.6 Summit.
- 34.5 Ride ends at Marin French Cheese Company.

9

Skaggs Springs Classic

Healdsburg—Dry Creek—Lake Sonoma—
Skaggs Springs—Cazadero—Monte Rio—
Guerneville—Rio Nido—Healdsburg

Elected Silence, sing to me/And beat upon my whorled
ear,/Pipe me to pastures still and be/The music that I care to
hear.
—Gerard Manley Hopkins, *"The Habit of Perfection"*

Think of Sonoma County and you're likely to envision miles of
electric green hills with ribbons of gnarled vines woven into their
undulations. Sonoma, the less touristy sister county to the famed
Napa, spreads over rich and varied countryside, rising to stony gray
peaks and dropping into fertile green valleys, stretching from the
sun-drenched Russian River to the rocky shores of the Pacific
Ocean. And while stately wineries and gently rolling country roads
are Sonoma's main attractions, most people don't even realize how
much more it has to offer. This tiny corner of the world is so deliciously fascinating that it seems almost imaginary. Could real life
possibly be this fantastical?

Your ride begins in downtown Healdsburg, a wine country community where you'll probably encounter more locals than tourists.
The town's hub of activity centers on a redwood-lined town square
that's filled with cafes and nouvelle cuisine restaurants. As you ride
out of town on Healdsburg Avenue, you'll pass the planned communities and schools of the Healdsburg residents before plunging
into the countryside in all its splendor. And when you cross under

Highway 101 on your bike, you make a symbolic gesture to the natural world: Nature promises you a gateway to some of its best-kept secrets. In return, you promise to leave the material worries of cars and office cubicles on the other side of that freeway.

The serpentine curves of Dry Creek Road provide an up-close communion with meticulously tended vineyards that roll along a brilliant green carpet. In the distance, hills swallowed by swarms of trees provide a foreshadowing of things to come. As the road gets narrower and traffic thins out, you leave the vineyards behind and forge onward to Lake Sonoma, where tourists, campers, and anglers alike come to frolic on the man-made (but quite lovely) lake.

From here a mega-climb awaits. It's the kind of ascent that, like a well-decorated fish story, will be elevated to legendary status just hours after you conquer it. But before that happens, you'll have to get through it. Do not succumb to the trickery of this climb. With its ridges that look so much like summits, it lures you into a false confidence, only to crush you mercilessly by revealing yet another uphill grade at the exact moment you thought you were done. But from the top, some 16 miles later, all the lung-burning, heart-pounding agony pays off. As you wipe the salt out of your eyes, you'll see hawks gliding low overhead and cows lolling in the clearing. The cold air and silent pasturelands make the warm valley vineyards, hidden in the folds of far-below hills, seem worlds away. For this moment chances are mighty good that you and your cycling partners will have the world to yourselves, and that you will have forgotten all about overcrowded cities and traffic jams. Chances are, you will have kept your pact with Nature.

The ecstasy of the summit is followed by miles of easy riding through unadulterated countryside and lush forests. The closer you get to the Pacific Ocean, the damper, darker, and mossier your surroundings become. But this ride is a study in contrasts, and as you veer away from the nearing ocean, the trees change dramatically, until you are once again amid idyllic pastureland, feeling like some character in a Wordsworth poem. You are alone as ever, except for cows lounging silently at the sides of the road and wandering aimlessly through deserted barns. Fences are unnecessary, for there is no reason to flee this beautiful place. Even the cows understand this.

The inevitable swooshing descent finally comes as the road spirals downward to Cazadero. After more than 50 miles of townless roads and nothing but the sounds of a rushing creek or a tree rustling in the breeze, you have once again reached civilization. Even so, except for a heavily trafficked stint on Highway 116, the roads, especially Austin Creek Road, are peaceful, gently nudging your tired limbs back to Healdsburg. And if the fertile soil and healthy souls of Healdsburg, Guerneville, and the Russian River are what civilization is all about, then, by God, it's not half-bad.

The Basics

Start: Intersection of Healdsburg Ave. and Matheson St. in downtown Healdsburg, north of Santa Rosa off Hwy. 101.
Length: 100.7 miles.
Terrain: Extended climbing, steeply graded ascents, rolling hills, some rough roads. Be in good shape!
Food: There are lots of cafes and restaurants in Healdsburg at the ride start/finish. Stock up on on-the-ride munchies in town, because you won't see another store until you reach Cazadero at mile 68.4. From then on there are plenty of markets, restaurants, and phones if you need to bail.
For more information: Lake Sonoma Recreation Area, 3333 Skaggs Springs Rd., Geyserville, CA 95441; (707) 433–9483.

Miles & Directions

- 0.0 Intersection of Healdsburg Ave. and Matheson St. in downtown Healdsburg. Head north on Healdsburg Ave. past the town square.
- 0.7 Road curves past a 7-Eleven; continue straight on Healdsburg Ave.
- 1.1 Left onto Dry Creek Rd.
- 1.4 Cross underneath Hwy. 101. Continue straight on Dry Creek Rd.

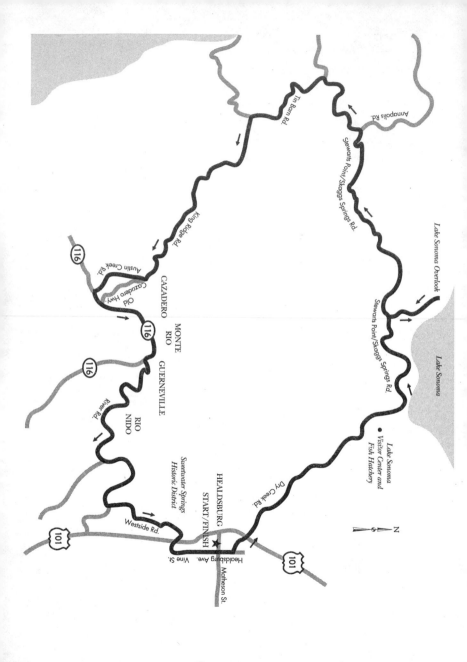

- 4.5 Dry Creek.
- 5.5 Dry Creek Rd. narrows.
- 11.9 Lake Sonoma Visitor Center and Fish Hatchery. Continue straight into the park.
- 12.2 Begin climbing.
- 13.7 Left on Stewarts Point/Skaggs Springs Rd. Follow signs TO OVERLOOK and TO MARINA.
- 14.2 Turn right for a quick side trip to Lake Sonoma Overlook; steep uphill grade.
- 14.7 Lake Sonoma Overlook.
- 15.1 Turn right back onto Stewarts Point/Skaggs Springs Rd.; continue climbing.
- 16.0 Short climbing reprieve.
- 17.4 Begin climbing again.
- 22.0 Summit.
- 26.2 Road becomes narrower and gravelly; begin another climb.
- 28.3 Summit.
- 41.0 Pass YMCA camp.
- 43.3 Pass Annapolis Rd. and old metal bridge; continue straight.
- 43.9 Cross one-lane bridge.
- 44.1 Begin climbing.
- 45.5 Summit. Left onto Tin Barn Rd.
- 51.4 Left onto King Ridge Rd. Follow sign TO CAZADERO.
- 60.0 Long descent begins; rough road.
- 67.8 Road diverges. Continue straight on main road.
- 68.1 Stop sign. Continue straight, following Cazadero Hwy.
- 68.4 Cazadero.
- 68.6 Veer onto Austin Creek Rd.
- 71.6 Austin Creek Rd. crosses Old Cazadero Hwy. Continue straight.
- 75.3 Left onto Hwy. 116 (River Rd.) to Monte Rio.
- 77.7 Monte Rio.
- 78.0 Stop sign; continue straight on River Rd.
- 82.2 Guerneville.
- 82.3 Stop sign; continue straight on River Rd.
- 83.9 Rio Nido.

- 85.2 Pass Korbel Winery.
- 87.7 Left onto Westside Rd.
- 90.7 Westside Rd. intersects with road to Santa Rosa; continue straight.
- 94.4 Pass Sweetwater Springs Historic District.
- 99.6 Pass W. Dry Creek Rd.; continue straight.
- 100.3 Cross under Hwy. 101; continue straight.
- 100.4 Healdsburg city limits.
- 100.5 Left onto Vine St.
- 100.7 Ride ends at intersection of Healdsburg Ave. and Matheson St.

10

Around and over
Diablo Classic

Walnut Creek—Clayton—Morgan Territory—
Danville—Mt. Diablo State Park—Walnut Creek

God made the grass, the air and the rain; and the grass, the
air and the rain made the Irish; and the Irish turned the
grass, the air and the rain back into God.
                                        —Sean O'Faolain, *Holiday*

It's a common experience among California bike tourists. You're
rolling beneath the shade of a dense forest when all of a sudden it
opens to naked rolling hills. In one fell swoop you've been transported to Ireland. And you are there, gliding over fog-enshrouded
hills, far away from everything American. Inevitable, inescapable
fantasizing begins. You, on a short ride home to your castle. You,
pedaling to the stone, ivy-covered mansion of your redheaded
love—just like the main character in some glorified Irish Spring
commercial. Even if you've never been to Ireland, the hills allow
you to transport yourself, and your imagination is able to let loose.

Marin County's Point Reyes is California's obvious Ireland
clone, but there are parts of Contra Costa County around the
foothills of venerable Mt. Diablo that also evoke that Ireland/Scot-
land wish-fulfillment-via-fantasy thing. It's hard to believe that the
Around and over Diablo Classic ride could ever lead to anything
pure if you judge it from its starting point in the quintessential suburb land of Walnut Creek. But after pedaling past the brand-new

housing developments in Clayton at mile 8, you come to the place where 1990s Americana stops and the ageless beauty of the natural world begins.

Turn onto Marsh Creek Road, and you are rolling past farmland on a virtually empty stretch of tarmac, where you're more likely to see a tractor than a car. Modest farmhouses with horses grazing in the front yards are scattered about the open grasslands, and your path becomes even more bucolic as you turn onto Morgan Territory Road, where gentle old trees form a shaded archway over the narrow road.

After 18 miles the road gets even skinnier and more remote. Trees thicken around you. For much of this stretch, the road is one-lane, so watch out for the occasional car that may twist unexpectedly around one of the snaky bends.

A gradual climb out of the trees yields to the Ireland-evoking open space of the Morgan Territory Regional Preserve. Lumpy green hills massage the earth, and weary bicyclists may feel a sense of renewal just from riding amid the pure quiet of the softly rolling hills. The air is sweet and clean and quiet, as tall, waving grass ripples in the wind. In just 24 miles of pedaling you've completely removed yourself from the material trappings of suburbia.

At mile 24.6 you'll pass rows of perfectly white, perfectly organized high-tech windmills covering the hillside to your left. Shortly afterward the road widens to two lanes and becomes a flat, winding ribbon carrying you past quiet countryside. In the distance Mt. Diablo rises high above the hills, waiting to torture your legs with its steep, unrelenting grades.

When you reach the Danville city limits, you'll have 5 miles of suburban riding—including a cruise through the sticky-sweet gingerbread houses and tennis villas of Blackhawk Road—before turning onto Diablo Scenic Drive, which marks your entrance into Mt. Diablo State Park. From here you'll have nearly 10 miles of climbing before reaching Diablo's summit. And 10 miles of mountain climbing can feel like dragging an anvil when you've already done 50 miles, especially on a hot day, when temperatures on Diablo's unshaded tarmac can be brutal.

Once you're atop Mt. Diablo, the pain of the climb is superseded by the victory of the conquest. On a clear day you can see much of the Bay Area spread out before you. And as the wind blows through your sweaty hair, you can look forward to the promise of 11 miles of scenic descending as you mount your two-wheeled companion and make your way back to Walnut Creek. From the bottom of Diablo, which ends with a no-brakes straightaway that provides the perfect culmination to this epic descent, you're only 5 miles from downtown Walnut Creek. Restaurants range from ethnic to the standard Big Three (McDonald's, Burger King, and Wendy's). And if celebrating the completion of a 73-mile ride means embracing the suburban lifestyle with a Biggie Coke and Biggie Fries, by all means, go for it.

The Basics

Start: Main St. and Civic St. in downtown Walnut Creek.
Length: 72.9 miles.
Terrain: Much extended climbing, rolling hills, some flat sections; moderate traffic in suburbs and towns but virtually no traffic for the majority of the ride.
Food: Restaurants and stores available in Walnut Creek. No food or water available for 30 miles between Clayton and Danville. Water fountains, but no food, on Mt. Diablo.
For more information: Valley Spokesmen Bicycle Touring Club, P.O. Box 2630, Dublin, CA 94568; Bonnie Powers, (415) 828–5299.

Miles & Directions

- ■ 0.0 Civic St. and Main St.; go south on Main St., away from downtown Walnut Creek.
- ■ 0.3 Right onto Ygnacio Blvd.; parallel bike path available.
- ■ 4.2 Bike path ends; climb begins.
- ■ 5.3 Summit.
- ■ 7.8 Right onto Clayton Rd.
- ■ 8.0 Clayton.

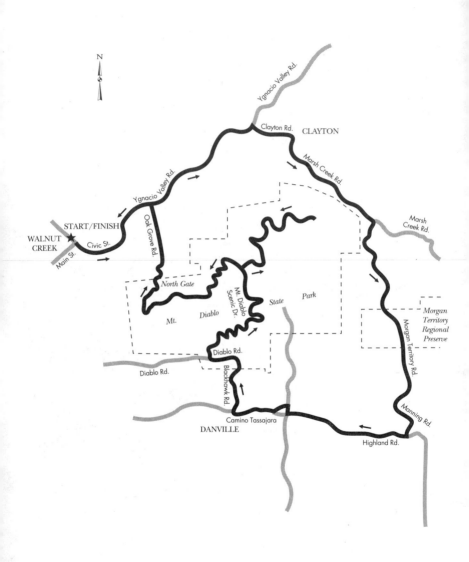

- 9.3 Right onto Marsh Creek Rd.
- 13.9 Right onto Morgan Territory Rd.
- 23.2 Morgan Territory Regional Preserve.
- 28.2 Alameda County line.
- 29.0 Right onto Manning Rd.
- 29.8 Right onto Highland Rd.
- 30.0 Contra Costa County line.
- 34.6 Right onto Camino Tassajara.
- 38.3 Danville town limits.
- 39.4 Right onto Blackhawk Rd.
- 43.0 Blackhawk Rd. becomes Diablo Rd.
- 43.1 Right onto Mt. Diablo Scenic Dr.; entrance to Mt. Diablo State Park.
- 43.9 Begin climbing.
- 50.1 Right to Mt. Diablo summit.
- 54.6 Summit; turnaround point.
- 59.1 Keep right at intersection, following North Gate.
- 67.1 Right onto Oak Grove Rd.
- 68.2 Left onto Ygnacio Valley Rd.
- 72.6 Left onto N. Main St.
- 72.9 Ride ends at Main St. and Civic St.

11

Sky Londa Cruise

*Downtown Palo Alto—Woodside—Old La Honda
Road—Sky Londa—Kings Mountain Road—
Woodside—downtown Palo Alto*

> *We think bicycles can save —if not the world—at least the
> quality of our immediate environments.*
> —1994 Bridgestone Catalogue

Palo Alto. Home to the brainy kids of Stanford University. Land of
the meticulously manicured yard. Gateway to God's Country.

With brains, wealth, and beauty to its credit, it's not surprising
that this idyllic setting is a full-on cycling mecca, where you can
find many a pair of fashionably buffed legs, watch a never-ending
parade of drool-evoking bikes, and discover myriad opportunities
for awe-inspiring cycling. Being that this is merely a touch of all
that Palo Alto and its surrounding areas have to offer, it's the perfect starting point for yet another killer ride.

A mix of coffee bars, restaurants, and bookstores complement
Palo Alto's downtown area, where the Wheelsmith Bike Shop and
Museum—voted one of the ten best bike shops in the country by
Bicycling magazine—offers the ideal launching pad for your cata-
pult into the surrounding hills.

From downtown Palo Alto the ride cruises through BMW and
Jaguar country, meanders across Stanford University, and lofts you
into the peaceful hills above Woodside, where you're immediately
distanced from the confusion below. Easter green in the spring and
classic brown in the summer, the hills are dotted with Christmas

tree farms, horse ranches, and elegant estates hidden among oak, birch, and redwood. Truly one of the more lovely parts of the Bay Area, these forested back roads come alive with Technicolor grandeur when you tour them by bike.

Once you turn onto Old La Honda Road, all traffic ceases, the road narrows, and your payoff begins. This tiny wooded road wriggles upward through the hills but never gets too steep to handle as it climbs for 3.5 miles to Skyline Boulevard (Highway 35). Expect to see fellow cyclists spinning and grinning under the shade of the towering trees that engulf the road and make it an absolute sanctuary in the summer. Once a logging road, Old La Honda narrows as you get closer to the summit, snaking precariously above the valley until you finally reach the top.

When you reach Skyline, you'll get to experience the rush of a screaming descent as you barrel into Sky Londa, a sparse smattering of civilization nestled quietly amid the redwoods. For hungry, weary cyclists ready for some real down-home cooking, you'll find Alice's Restaurant—a favorite hangout of bikers of the motorized variety. And for a quick food fix, there's a general store right across the street.

The ride continues on busy Highway 35, but not for long. After 5.8 miles of rolling hills, you'll turn onto quiet Kings Mountain Road. As it rambles through cooling redwood groves, this amazing sliver of asphalt includes dozens of hairpin turns that help to spiral the road downward to the valley. It's a tricky descent, so be sure to exercise caution. On your way down Kings Mountain Road, don't go so fast that you miss Huddart Park, one of the Peninsula's best-kept secrets (until now!). Take a quick look around and make a mental note to come back for a day hike and picnic.

Back on level ground in Woodside, you'll cruise past numerous horse farms, encountering not only four-legged beasts but also those of the four-wheeled variety. Yep. You're back to civilization, with all its grotesque (and glorious) trappings. Stop in at the well-to-do Woodside Market for a final pit stop, where you can mingle with the beautiful people before heading back to Palo Alto. Once you're back in town, Gordon Biersch, at 640 Emerson, serves up homemade brew and great food.

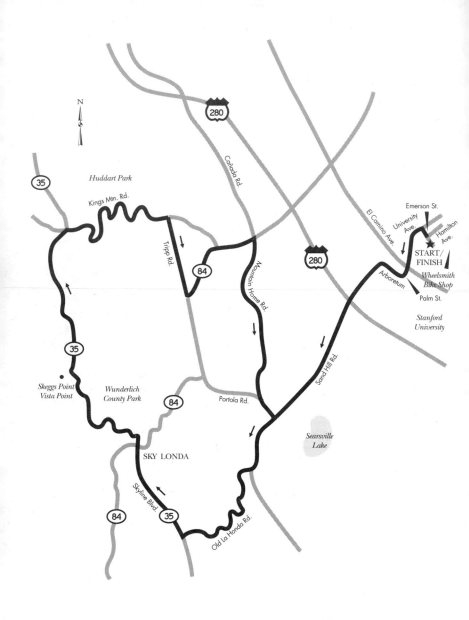

N

35

Huddart Park

Kings Mtn. Rd.

Cañada Rd.

280

Emerson St.

University Ave.

El Camino Ave.

Hamilton Ave.

Tripp Rd.

84

Mountain Home Rd.

280

START/
FINISH

Arboretum

Wheelsmith
Bike Shop

Palm St.

Stanford
University

35

Skeggs Point
Vista Point

Wunderlich
County Park

84

Portola Rd.

Sand Hill Rd.

Searsville
Lake

SKY LONDA

Skyline Blvd.

84

35

Old La Honda Rd.

The Basics

Start: Wheelsmith Bike Shop, Hamilton Ave. and Emerson St., downtown Palo Alto.

Length: 33.2 miles.

Terrain: Extended climbing on quiet backroads; moderate traffic between Woodside and Palo Alto.

Food: Myriad restaurants in Palo Alto; Alice's Restaurant and general store in Sky Londa; fancy restaurants and a grocery store in Woodside.

For more information: Western Wheelers Bicycle Club, P.O. Box 518, Palo Alto, CA 94302; Jim Evans, (415) 858–0936.

Miles & Directions

- 0.0 Wheelsmith Bike Shop, Hamilton Ave. and Emerson St. Head south on Emerson toward University Ave.
- 0.1 Left onto University Ave.
- 0.3 Cross El Camino Ave. University Ave. becomes Palm St.; enter Stanford University.
- 0.6 Right onto Arboretum.
- 1.0 Left onto Sand Hill Rd.
- 4.2 Cross Hwy. 280 overpass.
- 6.9 Right onto Old La Honda Rd. Begin climb.
- 10.5 Summit. Right onto Skyline Blvd. (Hwy. 35).
- 12.0 Intersection of Hwy. 35 and Hwy. 84. Continue on Hwy. 35 past Alice's Restaurant.
- 14.7 Wunderlich County Park.
- 16.0 Skeggs Point Vista Point.
- 17.8 Right onto Kings Mtn. Rd.
- 20.8 Huddart Park entrance.
- 22.3 Right at Woodside historical site, Tripp Rd.
- 23.1 Left onto Woodside Rd. (Hwy. 84).
- 24.4 Right onto Mountain Home Rd.
- 26.5 Left onto Portola Rd.
- 26.8 Left onto Sand Hill Rd.; retrace directions back to Palo Alto.
- 33.2 Ride ends at Wheelsmith Bike Shop.

12

Pinole Ramble

Pinole—Hercules—Rodeo—Crockett—Carquinez Scenic Drive—Carquinez Strait Regional Shoreline—Martinez—Alhambra Valley Road—Pinole

Thank goodness for cheap bicycles and the mass merchants who sell them. Inexpensive bicycles helped make childhood fun, and without them, lots of people would never have learned to ride a bike at all.

—1994 Bridgestone Catalogue

If you've got a bike (any bike will do) and you've got a body (any ole body), then you've got everything you need to enjoy this splendid ramble from the shores of the San Francisco Bay to the orchards of the Alhambra Valley. Cyclists new to the sport will love the Pinole Ramble as much as all the more experienced local riders who have made these delicious roads part of their regular cycling feast. On any given day you're likely to see everyone from the buffed-legs-and-fancy-bike set to the brand-new-bike-from-Kmart crowd out on their two-wheeled vehicles of choice, taking advantage of the less traveled roads around the Carquinez Strait and the Alhambra Valley.

Departing from the uninspiring suburb of Pinole, you'll find it hard to believe that you'll soon be traveling amid golden grasslands, wild groves of blackberries, and rolling farm roads. Of course, finding your way to these glorious Bay Area backroads takes a bit of perseverance. You'll have to battle the minimalls and golden arches of suburbia for 6 miles before your wheels roll onto the promised land. Included in this 6-mile tour-o'-the-'burbs is a grotesquely fascinating sensory extravaganza at the Wickland Oil Terminal. As you pedal by this monstrous structure, you can hear its clanging factory sounds, sniff its malodorous fumes, and behold its ugly industrial towers of pollution. It's a disturbing contrast to the glistening bay on your left, but for some sick reason it's hard to pull your eyes away from it.

Thankfully, cold suburbs and industrial wastelands are a thing of the past as you spin into the neighboring community of Crockett at mile 6.4. This cafe-and-thrift-store type of town doesn't have the impersonal glare of towns like Rodeo and Pinole. In fact, it has a certain good-natured funk to it. And best of all, it symbolizes your departure from the suburbs and your entrance into the sublime.

In less than 1 mile, your ride becomes countrified as you begin pedaling on the Carquinez Scenic Route. Because this route is not a through road for cars, you'll probably pass more walkers and cyclists than motorists.

As you wend through vast, undeveloped pasturelands, the threat of intense heat from this unshaded road is likely to be softened by cool air off the San Francisco Bay. As you rise and fall with the gentle pitches of road, the rush of wind and the expansive emptiness of the soft, lumpy hills are enough to evoke a near-perfect elation. The simple beauty of these grassy knolls that roll lazily to the shores of the Carquinez Strait serves as a reminder of what's really important in life.

When you encounter the road closure at mile 10.6, go around the gate and continue traveling on the Carquinez Scenic Route. The road is washed out, making it dangerous for cars but quite passable by bicycle. The absence of autos makes this short section of the route mystifyingly quiet. The fluttering of birds overhead and perhaps the whir of another bicycle wheel are the only sounds you'll hear. Watch for chunks of missing asphalt that disintegrate into dirt, and broken bits of road just waiting to puncture your tires. Your chances of flatting here are relatively high, and you won't want to be without your requisite tube, patch kit, and pump.

Rejoining cars and development in Martinez, you'll have a short jaunt through town, where you can stop for a snack before rejoining nature on the inland farm roads of the Alhambra Valley. You'll roll past wild blackberry patches, as well as rows of carefully planned orchards with tantalizing fruit dangling from their limbs. The road billows up and over soft green hills, as it snakes its way back toward Pinole, careening past full-on ranches and farms, and traversing alongside empty country meadows dotted with wildflowers.

After nearly 10 miles of pedaling on Alhambra Valley Road, you'll be reunited with the ever-lovin' fast-food restaurants and sacred shopping malls of America. But as you spin into Pinole, you'll be refueled with an insider's knowledge of the hidden beauty lying beyond the confines of these suburbs, the promise and hope inherent in an empty green hill or revealed in a patch of spontaneous wildflowers growing from the cracks of a quiet road. And this knowledge will carry you through until your next bike touring adventure.

The Basics

Start: San Pablo and Tennent Ave. intersection in downtown Pinole.

Length: 30.7 miles.

Terrain: Rolling hills, with a few extended climbs (no longer than 1 mile each). Quiet country roads for the majority of the ride.

Food: No grocery stores or restaurants at the ride start, but there's a big grocery store right on the bike route in the next town over, Hercules. After you've passed Crockett, there aren't any food options until you hit Martinez. From there you'll have the possibility of wild blackberries on Alhambra Valley Rd., but don't eat the farmers' fruit from their orchards, as tempting as it may be.

For more information: Valley Spokesmen Bicycle Touring Club, Box 2630, Dublin, CA 94568; Bonnie Powers, (415) 828–5299.

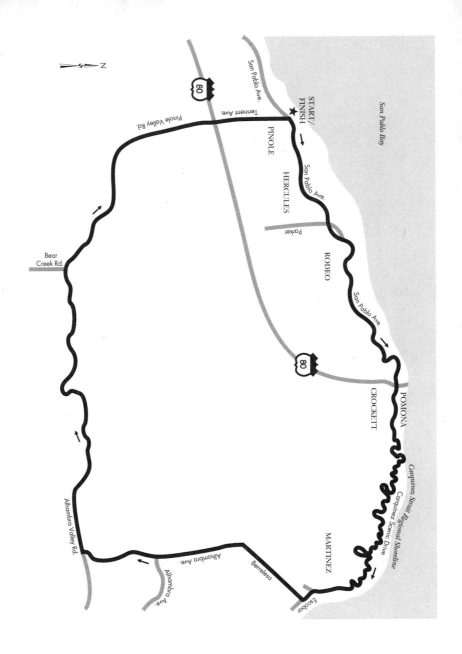

Miles & Directions

- 0.0 San Pablo Ave. and Tennent Ave. Turn right (east) onto San Pablo Ave. toward Hercules.
- 0.4 Hercules city limits.
- 2.3 Left onto Parker.
- 2.4 Rodeo city limits.
- 3.3 Parker becomes San Pablo Ave.
- 4.6 Wickland Oil Terminal. Begin climb.
- 5.5 Summit.
- 6.0 Crockett; San Pablo Ave. becomes Pomona.
- 6.1 Veer right; follow sign TO CARQUINEZ SCENIC DRIVE.
- 6.4 Downtown Crockett.
- 7.2 Begin Carquinez Scenic Dr.
- 8.3 Carquinez Strait Regional Shoreline.
- 10.6 Road closed (passable by bike).
- 14.5 St. Catherine of Siena Cemetery.
- 14.6 Carquinez Scenic Dr. becomes Talbart.
- 14.8 Veer left onto Escobar.
- 14.9 Right onto Berrelesa, which becomes Alhambra Ave.
- 16.9 Cross under Hwy. 4.
- 17.4 Right onto Alhambra Valley Rd.
- 18.7 Right at stop sign, continuing on Alhambra Valley Rd.
- 23.7 Intersect with Bear Creek Rd.; continue on Alhambra Valley Rd. to Pinole.
- 27.5 Pinole city limits. Alhambra Valley Rd. becomes Pinole Valley Rd.
- 30.0 Cross under Hwy. 80.
- 30.2 Pinole Valley Rd. becomes Tennent Ave.
- 30.7 Ride ends at Tennent Ave. and San Pablo Ave.

13

Headlands Loop Cruise

Fort Mason—Marina Green—
San Francisco Presidio—Golden Gate Bridge—
Marin Headlands—Fort Mason

East is East, and West is San Francisco, according to Cali-
fornians. Californians are a race of people; they are not
merely inhabitants of a state. They are the Southerners of
the West.

— William Sydney Porter, *A Municipal Report*

Bicycling in San Francisco is often like riding in the muddy gray
shades of a black-and-white television screen. The wind off the Pacific whips tears from your eyes, and fog hangs eerily over the city,
casting a gray shadow on even the brightest of colors. But hop on
your bike and pedal just a few miles over the Golden Gate Bridge
and your gray scale is magically transformed into the Technicolor,
sun-baked hues of Marin. It's at this moment—as the bridge's immense, brick-colored towers escort you away from the city—that
you'll be reminded of just how great it is to be riding in the diverse
state of California. As you reach the edge of the bridge, the Coastal
Mountain Range unfolds generously into the lapping shores of the
ocean. The fog has disappeared. The hills are innocent of development. You are pedaling into another perfect day in Marin County.
It's like being transported to another land, and the feeling is unde-
niably dramatic—as magical as the famed tornado that carried
Dorothy and Toto from Kansas to Oz.

While San Francisco is not always gray and Marin is not always blue, this is the general state of affairs—at least during the summer months. On any given weekend you'll see droves of cyclists making their mass exodus to Marin via that symbolic bridge of long departures and triumphant returns, the Golden Gate.

The Headlands Loop Cruise begins at Fort Mason Center, located on the very edge of San Francisco's Marina Green. This rectangular park stretches along the shores of the San Francisco Bay, from Fort Mason to the Presidio Army Base.

The Presidio is currently embroiled in the intricate legal process of transforming from army base to state park. From the verdant lawn of the Marina Green, you are dropped into an army base in the processes of abandonment. The stiff wind races through empty, boarded-up barracks lining Mason Street, giving it the impression of a military ghost town. Some troops are still on base, however, and you can see them meandering around in camouflage, blending right in with the tall, leafy eucalyptus trees that squeak creepily in the breeze. As you roll past the colorful pet cemetery and up the snaky Lincoln Drive, a string of increasingly beautiful vistas of the bay flaunt their conspicuous beauty. The Golden Gate Bridge, with its formidable red towers claiming much of the foreground, stands enmeshed amid the natural beauty of the sailboat-dotted bay, the immense Pacific Ocean, and Marin's soft hills.

Across the bridge your route dives into the hills of the Marin Headlands Golden Gate National Recreation Area and begins climbing. Conzelman Road twists above the Pacific Ocean, and before long you arc high above the bridge and city—and whatever stresses you may have felt are back on the other side of the bay. The climb is steep but relatively short, and the views of the ocean, the bay, the bridge, and the fair city of San Francisco far exceed the pain-and-sweat factor.

From the top you'll be treated to a swirling, drop-off-the-face-of-the-earth downhill that leads to the valley floor of the Headlands, as well as to the beach. Go slower than you think you need to. As you first drop down the other side, there's a steep hairpin turn just waiting to cause problems for inattentive cyclists. From the bottom of the hill, the options abound for cyclists wishing to explore the headlands. Turn left for a short jaunt out to the Point Bonita Lighthouse. Or make another left just past the visitor center to check out the beach. There's even a youth hostel with bunkbed accommodations for only $8.00 a night.

As Bunker Road begins its climb back to Conzelman, you'll understand why so many cyclists use these roads for training: hills. In fact, this is probably one of the toughest cruises listed in this book. No sooner have you patted yourself on the back for conquering Conzelman than you're back at it again. But one of the most charming aspects of this ride (depending on your mindset) is that it's short. When Bunker hits Conzelman, you're home free. It's basically downhill all the way back to the city, where you'll probably be needing that windbreaker you brought along.

The Basics

Start: Fort Mason Center, at Laguna St. and Marina Blvd. in San Francisco.
Length: 16.8 miles.
Terrain: Hilly roads; high traffic on weekends.
Food: Safeway supermarket at ride start; get snacks there, because there ain't no snack bars in the Headlands.
For more information: Golden Gate Cyclists, American Youth Hostels, 425 Divisadero, Suite 301, San Francisco, CA 94117; (415) 863–9939.

Miles & Directions

- 0.0 From Fort Mason Center, corner of Laguna St. and Marina St., head west to Golden Gate Bridge.
- 0.5 Enter Presidio; continue straight, following Mason St.
- 1.9 Left on Crissy Field Ave. at stop sign.
- 2.0 Right on Cowles St., just past pet cemetery.
- 2.2 Right on Lincoln Blvd.
- 2.6 Veer right onto bike path at Fort Point.
- 2.9 Follow sign directing you to the Golden Gate Bridge's left

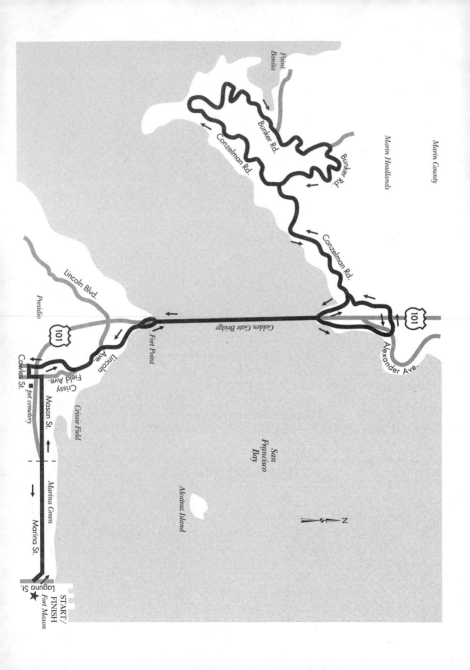

(west-side) bikeway/sidewalk on weekends and holidays, and to the right (east-side) bikeway/sidewalk on weekdays. (This route's mileage is calculated from the right side of the bridge, thus making it approximately 1 mile longer.)

- 4.1 Marin County line.
- 4.9 Cross Alexander Ave. and turn left, heading under subway.
- 5.2 Veer right toward Marin Headlands; begin climbing on Conzelman Rd.
- 6.2 Veer left, continuing upward on Conzelman Rd.
- 7.0 Summit.
- 7.1 Begin steep descent down Conzelman (one-way traffic, down only).
- 8.2 Veer right on Conzelman.
- 10.3 Right onto Bunker; begin climb.
- 11.6 Summit; left onto Conzelman.
- 12.6 Left onto service road, under subway; cross Alexander to Golden Gate Bridge bikeway.
- 13.2 Golden Gate Bridge.
- 14.9 Follow bike path back to Lincoln Ave.
- 15.2 Left onto Lincoln Ave.
- 15.6 Left onto Cowles.
- 15.8 Left onto Crissy Field Ave.
- 15.9 Right onto Mason.
- 16.3 Mason becomes Marina St.
- 16.8 Ride ends at Fort Mason Center.

Gold Country/
Cascades/Lake Tahoe

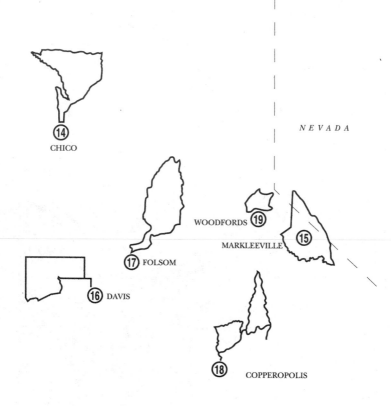

14 CHICO

N E V A D A

WOODFORDS **19**

MARKLEEVILLE **15**

17 FOLSOM

16 DAVIS

18 COPPEROPOLIS

Gold Country/Cascades/Lake Tahoe

14. Chico to Paradise Challenge 82
15. Monitor Pass Classic 87
16. Winters Farmland Cruise 92
17. Folsom Challenge 97
18. Calaveras County Challenge 102
19. Diamond Valley Ramble 106

Chico to Paradise Challenge

Chico—Paradise—Honey Run Road—
Bidwell Park—Chico

> *The cyclist-beer connection is undeniable. The true sign one*
> *has fully adapted to the cycling lifestyle is the endless quest*
> *for new and different beers, preferably of the micro-brewed*
> *variety.*
> —Henry Kingman, *California Bicyclist*

The remote town of Chico is perhaps best known for the media attention it's garnered as one of the country's top-ranking party schools. You'll find it nestled amid fiery canyons and undulating country roads—so seemingly unassuming, yet home to Chico State University, the bad boy of California's higher education system. The small town revolves around the school, and the school has given the town somewhat of a . . . reputation. There's no doubt that images of raucous frat boys and pitchers of cheap flat beer have discouraged more than one timid bike tourist or family-values type from planning a bike excursion in the area.

But don't let the media fool you. Cyclists in the know have long flocked to Chico for its small-town charm and quiet country roads and, of course, to hoist a few cool ones at the Sierra Nevada Brewery, which churns out one of the best local beers in the state. One look around at all the buffed legs and cool bikes in Chico and you'll understand why some visiting cyclists loved it so much that they never left.

Your ride begins in downtown Chico at Pullins Cyclery, a charming bike shop where classic Schwinns and state-of-the-art bikes share almost equal floor space. Best of all, there's none of that stereotypical, holier-than-thou bike shop attitude being copped at Pullins. And right across the street, you'll find the Chico Natural Foods store, where you can fuel up before embarking on your journey.

The Chico to Paradise Challenge is blessed with all the qualities that make for a perfect ride: the peace and solitude of less-traveled roads, varying terrain, incredible scenery, and a swooping descent that twists down one of the most gorgeous roads in all of America. But if you're visiting Chico in the summer, you'll want to do this ride in the early morning or late afternoon: Temperatures can easily soar above a hundred degrees in the warm months.

The first half of your ride is pancake-flat. You'll coast through shaded orchards and open farmland as the distant canyonlands draw nearer. With each passing mile their fiery hues become more brilliant—and their summits appear all the steeper.

After 19 miles of relative coasting, the climbing begins. If you can handle the 4-mile uphill grind, you'll be rewarded in Paradise—literally. The climb ends in a tiny hilltop town that carries this only slightly euphemistic name.

From there you'll follow rollercoaster hills to Honey Run Road, where a descent of mind-blowing proportions awaits. This 6-mile plummet is the granddaddy of highlights in a ride chock-full of minihighlights. The road leads to a covered bridge at Butte Creek, and you're likely to find other cyclists hanging out and taking in the view here before heading back to the confines of civilization. From the bridge it's a quick ride to the wooded trails of Bidwell Park, which will lead you back to downtown Chico and Pullins Cyclery. Here all the creature comforts necessary to fully bask in après-ride glow are right around the corner.

The Basics

Start: Pullins Cyclery, Main St. in downtown Chico.
Length: 46.5 miles.
Terrain: 19 miles of flat farmland on quiet country roads. One extended climb; one lengthy descent.

Food: Chico Natural Foods offers a great selection of organic produce and healthful snacks. Butte County Store at 14.1 miles has energy bars and more snacks. Back in Chico the food options abound.
For more information: Chico Velo Cycling Club, P.O. Box 2285, Chico, CA 95927; (916) 343–VELO.

Miles & Directions

- 0.0 From Pullins Cyclery, start where Main St. ends and Park Ave. begins.
- 1.5 Park Ave. and East Park Ave. intersect. Continue straight; Park Ave. becomes The Midway.
- 3.9 Veer left onto Oroville-Chico Hwy. **Careful:** It's easy to miss.
- 8.8 Doc's Restaurant, the only on-route restaurant until Paradise. **Warning:** Seedy and scary; only for the very brave.
- 8.9 Oroville-Chico Hwy. ends at Durham-Dayton Hwy. Left onto Durham-Dayton Hwy.
- 9.4 Cross over Hwy. 99; becomes Durham-Pentz Rd.
- 13.2 Butte College.
- 14.1 Cross Clark Rd. (Hwy. 191) to Butte County Store: Stock up on food, Power Bars, water, etc. Continue on Durham-Dayton Hwy., now called Durham-Pentz Rd.
- 18.2 Durham-Pentz Rd. ends at Pentz Rd. Left onto Pentz Rd.
- 19.0 Climb begins.
- 23.8 Paradise city limits; food and water available.
- 25.0 Left onto Pearson Rd.; rollercoaster hills—have fun!
- 28.5 Pearson Rd. ends at The Skyway. Turn right onto The Skyway.
- 28.6 Left onto Honey Run Rd. **Caution:** Steep and bumpy descent on twisty one-lane road. Wear gloves and watch for cars.
- 32.2 Honey Run Rd. widens to two lanes.
- 34.3 Covered bridge at Butte Creek. Veer left and continue on Honey Run Rd.
- 38.7 Right onto The Skyway. Back to civilization.
- 39.5 Right onto Bruce Rd.; Bruce Rd. becomes Manzanita.

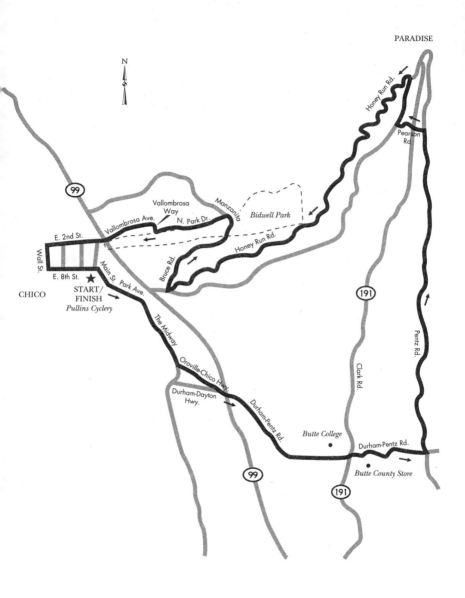

N

PARADISE

Honey Run Rd.

Pearson Rd.

99

Vallombrosa Way
Vallombrosa Ave.
N. Park Dr.
Manzanita
Bidwell Park
E. 2nd St.
Honey Run Rd.
Wall St.
Bruce Rd.
E. 8th St.
CHICO
START/
FINISH
Pullins Cyclery
Main St.
Park Ave.

191

Pentz Rd.

The Midway

Oroville-Chico Hwy.

Durham-Dayton
Hwy.

Durham-Pentz Rd.

Clark Rd.

Butte College

Durham-Pentz Rd.

99

Butte County Store

191

- 42.9 Left onto Vallombrosa Ave.
- 43.1 Left onto N. Park Dr.
- 45.4 Swimming hole at "One Mile." Turn right onto Vallombrosa Way; then make an immediate left onto Vallombrosa Ave.
- 46.0 Vallombrosa Ave. becomes E. 2nd St.
- 46.0 Left onto Wall St.
- 46.4 Right onto E. 8th St.
- 46.5 Ride ends at Main St. and Pullins Cyclery.

15

Monitor Pass Classic

Woodfords—Markleeville—Monitor Pass—Topaz Lake—Gardnerville, Nevada—Minden, Nevada— Centerville, Nevada—Woodfords

They're out there every weekend. As soon as the snow melts, they're out there.
—Markleeville resident, overheard in Tiers of Joy cafe

When you see them all out there, clad in their electric yellow windbreakers and gnawing on their Power Bars, you have to wonder, "Am I one of them?" Even if you sport the same gear, wear the same clothes, and drink the same powdered substances, there's something about seeing them all out there, sweating up mountains in a majestically pristine setting. It feels a bit funny—like you're not as different as you thought you were.

Are you one of them? The answer, of course, is yes. Anyone who's gone to the extreme of buying this book—and anyone who's even *thinking* about tackling Monitor Pass, the famed Markleeville Death Ride's toughest of five mountain climbs—is one of them.

And while it may seem a bit strange to see all your newfound bikie brothers and sisters out on the same remote roads on a non-century day, it's also a bonding experience. They've all been riding up and down the same mountains that you are going to ride. They have sweated on the same roads. They have grunted around the same steep switchbacks.

This is Alpine County, home of the much-heralded Death Ride, where thousands of cyclists convene once a year to push their limits up five mountain passes and over 130 miles. But since it has received so much press, bicycling in Alpine County is no longer limited to one hyped-up day. Death Riders are out tackling these roads all summer long.

The Monitor Pass Classic charts a formidable and diverse route by starting in Woodfords (also the start/finish of the Diamond Valley Ramble), climbing the toughest of Alpine County's mountain passes, and then traveling onward to Nevada before eventually wending its way back to Woodfords. The actual Death Ride travels over both sides of Monitor as well as Ebbetts, Luther, and Carson passes. If you dare try all five passes, a detailed map of the area will help you plot the route. Or better yet, sign up for the ride—which fills up fast—by contacting the Alpine County Chamber of Commerce at the number on page 89.

Six miles of rolling hills get you from Woodfords to Markleeville, where cafes, delis, and a general store form a two-block town. Stop in one of the stores and tell the person behind the counter what you're about to do. In other small mountain towns, people would say you were crazy; they'd warn you not to try it. Here they don't bat an eye. They've seen it all before. They understand our kind.

Continuing past Markleeville, you'll begin ascending alongside Monitor Creek at a relatively moderate rate. **Caution:** Don't be tricked into thinking you've begun your climb up Monitor. You ain't seen nuthin' yet. The climbing begins in earnest when you turn left at the sign TO MONITOR PASS—and it doesn't let up until you reach the top, 9.6 miles later. In fact, it seems to get harder the higher you go. Is it really getting steeper, or is the altitude beating you down? Or could it be that the never-ending 10 percent grades are crushing your mortal legs?

All of these things would be important were it not for the incredible views your pain affords you. Had you stayed on the porch of the general store in Markleeville (a tempting alternative), you would have missed the lush high-alpine meadows, the shimmering leaves of the aspen, the white, peely bark of the birch, the rough and rocky terrain of the mountain, and the incredible mountaintop vistas of a far-below valley floor stretching from California to

Nevada. Had you stayed in Markleeville, you would have missed the thrill of climbing to 8,314 feet—and the ecstasy of a lusciously steep, well-deserved descent.

Shortly after reaching the bottom of Monitor and turning onto Highway 395, you'll pass Topaz Lake and cross the Nevada state line. It's browner and flatter here, but fascinating in its own right. Mountains spring up from the flat earth with no trace of a foothill. Signs for places like Sharkey's Casino remind you that you're no longer in California. The Carson Valley Bike Center, housed in an Old West building featuring a wooden clapboard front porch with antique bikes hanging from its rafters, is a pleasant surprise in the smallish town of Minden.

As you turn onto Highway 88, the snowy peaks of the Sierra Nevadas loom larger in the foreground, and before you know it, you're back in California, where everything seems to magically become more lush. More dramatic. More serene. And best of all, from the state line Woodfords is just 6 easy miles away.

The Basics

Start: Intersection of Hwy. 88 and Hwy. 89 in Woodfords.
Length: 71.1 miles
Terrain: Steep mountain climbing, lots of rolling hills; low traffic in California, moderate traffic on Hwy. 395 in Nevada.
Food: General stores in Woodfords and Markleeville; no food from Markleeville to Nevada; many food options in Gardnerville and Minden.
For more information: Alpine County Chamber of Commerce, P.O. Box 265, Markleeville, CA 96120; (916) 694–2475.

Miles & Directions

- 0.0 From the intersection of Hwy. 88 and Hwy 89. in Woodfords, turn right onto Hwy. 89 toward Markleeville.
- 6.2 Markleeville city limits.

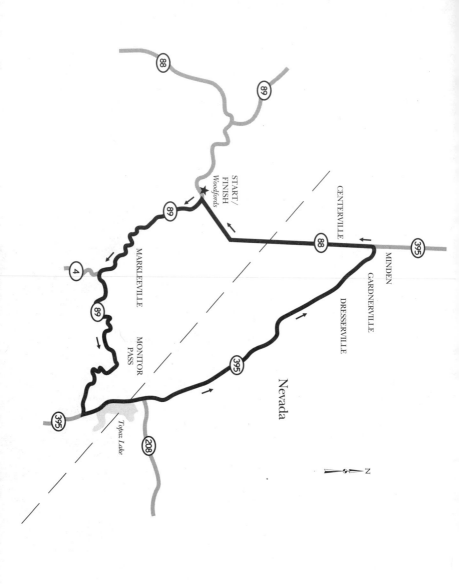

- 11.4 Left at Monitor Pass.
- 20.0 Monitor Pass.
- 21.6 Enter Mono County.
- 29.3 Left onto Hwy. 395.
- 30.5 Topaz Lake.
- 32.5 Nevada state line.
- 35.7 Intersection of Hwy. 395 and Hwy. 208.
- 54.0 Gardnerville.
- 55.5 Minden.
- 56.9 Left at Hwy. 88.
- 60.3 Centerville.
- 64.9 California state line.
- 70.8 Woodfords city limits.
- 71.1 Ride ends at intersection of Hwy. 88 and Hwy. 89.

16

Winters Farmland Cruise

Davis—Putah Creek Road—Winters—Davis

> O beautiful for spacious skies,/For amber waves of grain,/For
> purple mountain majesties/Above the fruited plain!
> —Katharine Lee Bates, "America the Beautiful!"

Flat. As a pancake. As a desert plain. As a lovebug on your windshield. Flat. Dead flat. The Winters Farmland Cruise is undoubtedly the most level ride in this entire book. The roads on this tour undulate about as much as a starched shirt on Wall Street.

But this ride is far from flat in terms of scenery. Hellaciously hot in the summer and enshrouded with fog in the winter, the roads around Davis provide a gateway into America's heartland. You'll pedal right past those oft-heralded amber fields of grain with a backdrop of majestic purple mountains outlining the distance.

The ride begins in downtown Davis, a small agribusiness/college town just down the road apiece from Sacramento. As close as it is to sprawling Sacto, the city of Davis is no suburb. It has a funky, collegiate feel, complete with espresso bars, vegetarian restaurants, and bikes galore. And due to its pancakelike pavement, many of the bikes you'll see are retro Schwinn cruiser types—embellished with flower-laced handlebar baskets—used mainly for the purpose of commuting about town.

From the ride's start at Wheelworks bike shop, you'll take to tree-lined Russel Street, which in the summer provides a touch of shade from Davis's unrelenting heat. But cover from the rays is only a temporary luxury. Within 2 miles the road yields to vast, open farmland with miles of crops plotted on meticulously tilled land. The rhythm of symmetrically planted rows is eventually broken at mile 7.4 by a stone bridge covered with a blanket of graffiti. With its multicolored rainbows and swirls, this vivacious structure can bring a smile to even the sternest of mouths, giving rise to the argument that maybe sometimes—just sometimes—graffiti can actually be a beautification process.

But after you cross the bridge, it's back to the fields. As you turn onto Putah Creek Road, the often still air and always empty roads—combined with the symmetry of the rows of crops—can feel almost spooky, as if you could be the next victim in a *Children of the Corn* movie or something. If your imagination is running wild, you can amuse yourself otherwise by trying to guess what the farmers are growing. One mile yields leafy little bushes erupting from mounds of brown earth. But pedal another mile and you're passing orchards of almonds and apples growing in carefully planned abundance.

After 14 miles of flat farmland, you'll get a few rollers as you head into Winters. A few, mind you. And certainly nothing to shake a stick at. These are your only "hills" for the day, so make what you will of them. Cross Putah Creek and you're rolling into the farming community of Winters, a small and welcoming town with a few sincere restaurants, a large feed and seed store and less than a dozen blocks of modest homes.

From your Winters vantage point, the distant mountains are drawn nearer. Lofting on the horizon, these peaks are still far enough away that you can enjoy their scenic merits instead of worrying about an impending climb.

A stoic white barn marks your turn onto Road 27—no real need for cutesy names like Almond Orchard Avenue out here. Even the roads are plotted meticulously, forming a series of grids that mirror the crops in between them and making it incredibly difficult to get lost. To get back to Davis, just keep making right turns.

On your way back to Davis, a few barren, twisted trees stand alone in the fields with their branches outstretched like an old witch's hand. Adding to this eerie scene, a run-down mansion is perched awkwardly on the side of the road, marking your final turn onto Road 99 back toward town. The once-regal house seems to be rotting from within, yet it has an obvious psychedelic air coursing through it, as if it's now inhabited by Deadheads/UC Davis students.

From here you'll have 8 more flat miles back to town. Once there, you'll find the Tutti Cafe located conveniently next to the bike shop. Park your bike amid the cruisers and treat yourself to an iced tea, or mill around the well-stocked bike shop. If you're feeling brave, ask the salespeople about another great Davis ride—the Davis Double. If your Winters Farmland Cruise was too easy, you might just love the Davis Double. Sponsored by the Davis Bike Club, this well-attended ride covers 200 miles in one day, and this time you'll make it to those majestic purple mountains. Ouch!

The Basics

Start: Wheelworks Bike Shop, 3rd St. and F St., downtown Davis.
Length: 40.7 miles.
Terrain: Flat, quiet farm roads.
Food: The Blue Mango Cafe in downtown Davis has great vegetarian meals; the Davis Co-op at 6th and G streets has just about everything you'll need for a midride picnic or on-the-bike snacks; and there's a general store in Winters if you need a quick fix.
For more information: Davis Bike Club, 336 Del Oro, Davis, CA 95616; DBC Hotline, (916) 756–0186.

Miles & Directions

- 0.0 Wheelworks bike shop, 3rd St. and F St. Go north on 3rd St.
- 0.2 Left onto 5th St.
- 0.6 UC Davis. Fifth St. becomes Russel; bike path available.
- 1.7 Cross over Hwy. 113.
- 6.6 Bike path ends at three-way intersection; sharp left onto Rd. 95A, unmarked.
- 8.0 Right onto Putah Creek Rd.

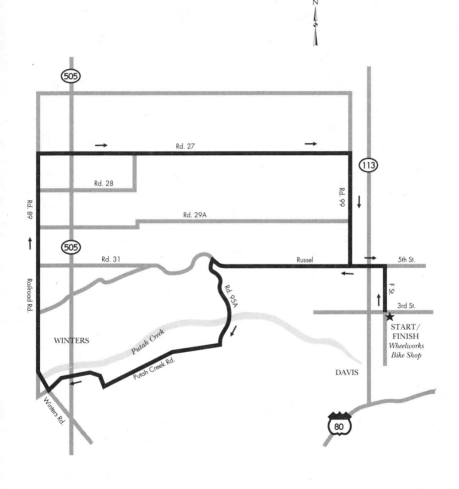

- 14.3 Cross under overpass; follow sign TO WINTERS.
- 15.2 Right onto Winters Rd.; cross Putah Creek bridge.
- 15.3 Winters. Winters Rd. becomes Railroad Rd. and eventually becomes Rd. 89.
- 22.4 Right onto Rd. 27.
- 23.5 Cross Hwy. 505.
- 32.7 Right onto Rd. 99.
- 36.8 Davis city limits. Rd. 99 becomes Lake.
- 37.9 Left onto Russel; bike path available.
- 39.0 Cross Hwy. 113.
- 40.1 Russel becomes 5th St.
- 40.6 Right onto F St.
- 40.7 Ride ends at 3rd St. and F St.

17

Folsom Challenge

Folsom—American River Parkway—Auburn—Cool—
Pilot Hill—Salmon Falls Road—Folsom

> *A bike God is a talisman. It is something you can only get*
> *when you are riding. It must be a gift of the journey. You*
> *can't buy it. You can't know what it is before you get it. It*
> *just comes.*
>
> —Mark Jenkins, *Off the Map*

In the oft-divisive cycling world, some see bike paths as the blessed, two-wheeled solution to overcrowded city streets, whereas others view them as part of a mastermind conspiracy to keep bicycles off the road. Are bike riders being handed the recycled rhetoric of the pre–civil rights, down-South, separate-but-equal dogma? Or do we even *want* to share the roads with smelly, obnoxious cars?

A heady, often heated discussion, to be sure. But no matter what side of the symbolic bike path you fall on, there are some paths that are just too pretty to pass up. Such is the case with Folsom's American River Parkway, the starting place for the Folsom Challenge. Even if you hate the idea of bike paths, toss your principles aside for just a few hours and try this 8-mile stretch of the 38-mile American River Parkway, which actually originates way back in Sacramento. Arguably the most scenic part of the entire bike path, the route meanders through the quiet hills of Folsom and alongside the banks of Lake Natoma. And if the scenery doesn't convince you, there's always the promise of a cheap ego boost—because no matter how slow you are, bike paths usually provide at least a few kids on tricycles for you to pass.

The bike path parallels Auburn-Folsom Road, which you'll be filtered onto after 8 miles on the bike path. From here you'll have to deal with cars and hills as you make your way to Auburn, but the scenery along the tree-lined road is relaxing, with the white fences of horse ranches bordering the road and the ornate gates of ritzy planned communities popping up every now and then.

After 23 miles of riding, you reach Auburn and are treated almost immediately to a swooping, spiraling descent that twists through fiery canyons and drops down to the rushing north fork of the American River. In a matter of minutes, the minimalls of Auburn have been left behind and you are dwarfed by the rocky foothills of the gold-rush mountains that continue to grow in size and proportion from here all the way to Lake Tahoe. A deep green bridge arches high above in the distant sky, poised majestically amid mountains.

From here there's nowhere to go but up. After following Highway 49 across the American River, you'll be faced with a steep and writhing climb up a skinny road cut deep into the side of the mountain. Shoulders are virtually nonexistent here, and there are a few serious blind spots, so ascend with caution. Although the climb is only 2 miles, the top comes just in the nick of time for most legs. From here the foliage becomes greener and the road transcends from a harsh, mountain-hugging challenge to a rollicking romp through pleasantly rolling fields.

These gentle hills mark your entrance into the tiny town of Cool, where you can get a snack at the general store and be on your way. This blink-and-you'll-miss-it burg boasts beautiful vast pastureland, and only a few slight buildings. There's not much to do out here except ride—which, of course, makes the riding near-perfect. You'll roll along for 4 more miles before hitting Pilot Hill and turning off, right after the gas station, onto the unmarked Salmon Falls Road. After dealing with one more brief climb, you'll be treated to miles of luscious, uninterrupted descending through verdant hillsides thick with trees and glorious rust-colored canyons. Gorgeous valley vistas greet you around almost every bend. Salmon Falls Road typifies cycling at its flawless, inspiring best: It's roads like this that renew cyclists' passion for the sport and invigorate our souls.

You'll have 10 miles of countryside before plopping down in the outskirts of Folsom. And at mile 51 you'll pass Folsom Prison—the same one that Johnny Cash made famous with "Folsom Prison Blues," crooning that he "shot a man in Reno, just to watch him die." Don't loiter for long along this stretch of road, lest your intentions be misconstrued by prison authorities. From here it's a quick, easy ride back to the American River Parkway where the ride began.

The Basics

Start: Hazel Ave. and Gold Rush Ave., at Lake Natoma, near the American River Parkway in Folsom.
Length: 57 miles.
Terrain: Steep climbs, lots of rollers and gentle uphill grades, some flat sections; moderate to heavy traffic for 2-mile climb on Hwy. 49 and on Auburn-Folsom Rd.
Food: No food at the ride's start; stores available in Auburn at mile 23 and in Cool at mile 30.
For more information: Sacramento Wheelmen, 920 27th St., Sacramento, CA 95815; Trudy Johnson, (916) 444–8577.

Miles & Directions

- 0.0 Hazel Ave. and Gold Country Rd. Follow Hazel Ave. across the bridge to American River Pkwy.
- 0.2 Right onto American River Pkwy.; veer left at the bottom of the hill.
- 8.4 Bike path veers right to snack bar (0.1-mile detour); turn left onto Park Rd.
- 8.5 Park entrance.
- 8.7 Right onto Auburn-Folsom Rd.
- 20.5 Auburn city limits.

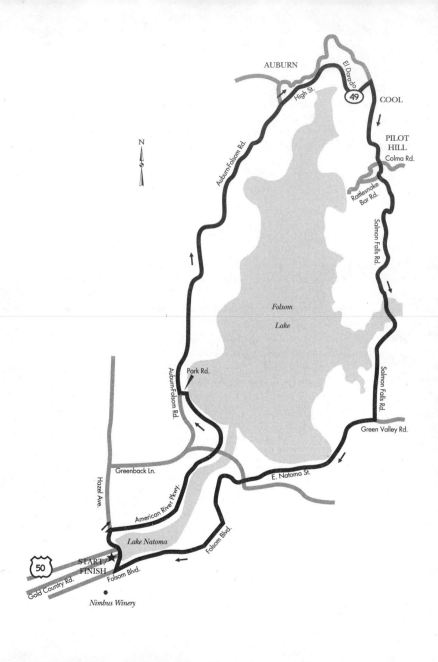

- 23.4 Right onto High St.
- 24.4 High St. becomes El Dorado (Hwy. 49); begin twisty descent.
- 26.7 Turn right onto bridge at bottom of descent; follow sign TO COOL.
- 26.8 Begin steep climb.
- 28.7 Summit.
- 30.1 Cool city limits.
- 33.6 Pilot Hill. Go straight past Rattlesnake Bar Rd. and Pilot Hill gas station.
- 34.0 Right onto Salmon Falls Rd. (unmarked).
- 34.1 Left at stop sign.
- 45.8 Right onto Green Valley Rd.
- 48.8 Right onto E. Natoma St.
- 51.0 Folsom State Prison.
- 52.5 Left onto Folsom Blvd.
- 56.4 Right onto Hazel Ave. at Nimbus Winery.
- 57.0 Ride ends at Hazel Ave. and Gold Country Rd.

18

Calaveras County Challenge

Copperopolis—Felix—Pool Station—San Andreas—
Angels Camp—Copperopolis

> *He'd give him a little punch behind, and the next minute*
> *you'd see that frog whirling in the air like a doughnut—see*
> *him turn one summerset, or maybe a couple if he got a good*
> *start, and come down flat-footed and all right, like a cat.*
> —Mark Twain, *"The Celebrated Jumping Frog*
> *of Calaveras County"*

Mark Twain spent only three years of his life in California's Gold Country, but in that time he put himself and the area on the map with his first big story, *"The Celebrated Jumping Frog of Calaveras County."* And even today people there haven't forgotten him. Everywhere you go, you run into places like the Mark Twain Mini Mall or the Twain Super Six Movie Theatre. In Angels Camp frog icons pop up everywhere, an annual jumping frog contest and festival are still held, and the legend of the cantankerous genius that was Mark Twain lives on.

The Calaveras County Challenge heads out to the delightful burg of Angels Camp via some of the finest backroads in all of California. Starting in the nowheresville town of Copperopolis, the cycling is immediately rural and peaceful. Along rolling country roads sit lonely farmhouses plotted on miles of open space. Oak trees with branches arching lazily toward the earth spring from the folds of the hills, and solitary cows graze in pastoral bliss amid the vast open fields.

As you meander through the hilly countryside, cars and houses become fewer and farther between, and roads with no names or signs are common, making it easy for the first-time bike tourist to get confused. The trickiest section comes when you reach the small cluster of farmhouses at mile 6.8. Your main road seems to veer off to the left, but you should continue straight past the farms. You'll be heading toward the hills on a road so jarring that you can feel every crack and cranny of its broken asphalt. Thankfully, the surface improves as the first real climb begins, at mile 8.8 on Hunt Road. As you twist upward through the countryside, the soft outline of the Sierra Nevadas appears on the horizon and all the heart-pounding agony seems worthwhile.

As you drop down to Pool Station, you'll turn off onto Pool Station Road, where golden wildflowers blanket the soft hills for much of the year and the branches of oak trees swoop down to shade the road on hot summer days. Another 2-mile climb awaits you at mile 23.4, and the terrain becomes more rocky as you pass a jagged reservoir before summiting and heading downward to the town of San Andreas and the moderately busy Highway 49. Here you'll find numerous food options and B&Bs, making it a great place to take a break—or the perfect home base for a weekend of bike exploring.

Ride for just over 8 more miles and you'll reach Angels Camp, where you can relive all the Twain lore, visit a nineteenth-century schoolhouse, and groove to the Old West atmosphere that permeates the historic downtown. You'll definitely want to venture past Highway 4 and check out the historic old town, which is just a few miles down the main road. When you've had your fill, turn around and head back to Highway 4, where you'll have a hilly 10 miles back to Copperopolis.

The Basics

Start: McCarty's Copper Inn, Copperopolis, located off Hwy. 4, which can be accessed from Hwy. 5 in Stockton.
Length: 52.4 miles.
Terrain: Rolling roads, with some extended climbing; mostly quiet backroads with little traffic; some rough surfaces.

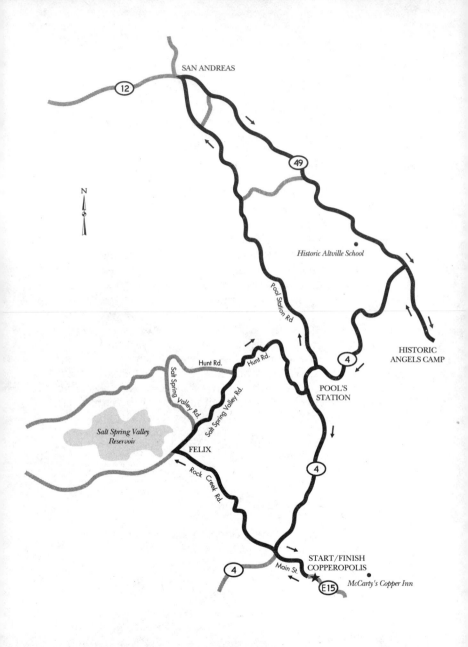

N

SAN ANDREAS

12

49

Historic Altville School

Pool Station Rd.

HISTORIC
ANGELS CAMP

4

POOL'S
STATION

Hunt Rd.

Hunt Rd.

Salt Spring Valley Rd.

Salt Spring Valley Rd.

Salt Spring Valley
Reservoir

FELIX

4

Rock Creek Rd.

4

Main St.

START/FINISH
COPPEROPOLIS

E15

McCarty's Copper Inn

Food: McCarty's Copper Inn has energy bars and myriad other snacks to get you started. You won't have another chance to refuel until you reach San Andreas at mile 28.8.

For more information: Calaveras County Chamber of Commerce, 3 North Main Street, San Andreas, CA 95249 (209) 754–4009.

Miles & Directions

- 0.0 From McCarty's Copper Inn turn left onto Main St. toward Hwy. 4.
- 0.5 Cross Hwy. 4; go straight on Rock Creek Rd.
- 6.6 Road Ts; turn right onto Salt Spring Valley Rd.
- 6.8 Straight past unmarked road, then through gate, past farmhouses toward hills.
- 8.8 Salt Spring Valley Rd. intersects with Hunt Rd., then becomes Hunt Rd. Continue straight and begin climb.
- 12.2 Begin descent.
- 12.5 Left onto Hwy. 4.
- 13.2 Left onto Pool Station Rd.
- 23.4 Begin climb.
- 25.3 Summit.
- 28.8 Right onto Hwy. 49 (unmarked); San Andreas.
- 37.0 Angels Camp city limits.
- 37.6 Historic Altaville school.
- 39.8 Historic Angels Camp.
- 40.7 Left onto Hwy. 4 west to Copperopolis. (Mileage varies here, depending on how far into town you went.)
- 51.9 Left onto Main Street in Copperopolis.
- 52.4 Ride ends at McCarty's Copper Inn.

19

Diamond Valley Ramble

Woodfords—Diamond Valley—Woodfords

A ride is a ride, not a mission, not a race, not an end in itself.
—Maynard Hershon, *California Bicyclist*

Seems the more you ride, the more you begin to accept suffering into your life as part of the whole cycling deal. You begin to seek out the highest peaks and the ultradistance rides. But in the middle of nowhere, with no hills to worry about, no nervous spasms at the thought of 80 more miles to go, no cars threatening your life as they whiz by at 75 miles per hour, your bike suffering factor becomes virtually nil. And with hardship out of the way, you are freed up to check out the scenery, savor the quiet—maybe even think deep thoughts, ponder the meaning of life, and so forth. The ride becomes secondary, because it's so carefree that you don't even have to think about it.

While hardcore riders may argue that suffering is precisely the tool necessary to lead body and mind to heights of greatness, the 12-mile Diamond Valley Ramble offers strong evidence that a short, flat ride can, under the right circumstances, be just as beautiful, just as enlightening, as a 150-mile gruelathon.

The Diamond Valley Ramble is one of two Alpine County rides that start and end in Woodfords and are featured in this book. Along with rustic lodges and cabins aplenty, there are thirteen campgrounds in Alpine County alone, and even more in the surrounding areas. Facilities range from primitive (a.k.a. fewer people) to fully equipped with showers and flush toilets (read: Winnebagos, kids, Doritos). Spend the weekend here and tackle both the Diamond Valley Ramble and the Monitor Pass Classic, or leave the classic to your more aggressive partners and take to exploring the less traveled roads of Diamond Valley—there's more to see than what's on this route slip; all you need is a map.

Leaving from Woodfords, your ride starts with a short, steep pitch of road as you climb up Highway 89 to your turnoff at Diamond Valley Road. Once your wheels hit this thin ribbon of tarmac, all cars disappear and the quiet countryside takes over. Get about 1 mile away from Highway 89 and you are utterly alone. There are no campgrounds, no homes—not even an abandoned shack. The potent smell of wildflowers wafts through the air as the scenery alternates from pastoral meadows to scrubby bushes and barren hills—all cradled by the sylvan, snow-covered peaks of the Sierra Nevadas. As you ride through on your two-wheeled steed, it all feels very Old West in a Hollywood kind of way. You almost expect to see a pair of rugged pioneers/cowboys crest one of the hills atop their horses.

But you are reminded of the realities of the 1990s when you come across the Hung-a-Lel-Ti southern band of the Washoe tribe of California-Nevada, at mile 5.2. From outward appearances, these are not the Native Americans of history books or Hollywood movies, but the modern-day victims of a nation that's forgotten them. This barren patch of land is what the government has given them to call home. And there are no tepees and horses, only modest residences and broken-down cars.

As Diamond Valley Road curls around this small reservation, you can alter the published ride by taking Long Valley Road (which becomes Indian Creek Road when you cross the Nevada state line) all the way to the larger Washoe reservation in Dresserville. From there you can hook up with Highway 395, which intersects with Highway 88 in Minden and heads back to Woodfords.

Continuing past the reservation, your route crosses Highway 88 and leads to yet another stone-quiet section of riding along Emigrant Trail, a paved road that follows a small portion of the historic route forged by the bold travelers of California's gold rush of 1848. The road rolls along the foothills of the Sierra Nevadas, delivering you all the way back to Woodfords. There you can pick up a snack

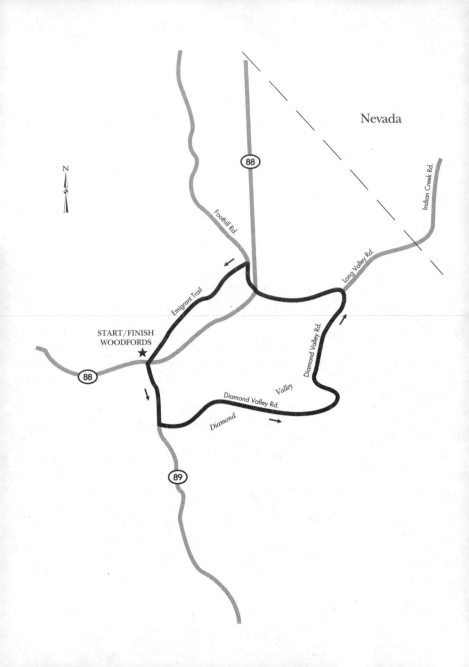

at the general store and enjoy the serenity of life in the mountains of Alpine County, California's least populated—and perhaps most beautiful—county.

The Basics

Start: Intersection of Highway 88 and Highway 89 in Woodfords.
Length: 12 miles
Terrain: Mostly flat; some rolling hills; virtually carless roads.
Food: General store in Woodfords; no food available on ride.
For more information: Alpine County Chamber of Commerce, P.O. Box 265, Markleeville, CA 96120; (916) 694–2475.

Miles & Directions

- 0.0 From the intersection of Hwy. 88 and Highway 89 in Woodfords, turn right onto Hwy. 89 toward Markleeville.
- 0.5 Left onto Diamond Valley Rd.
- 5.2 Hung-a-Lel-Ti, southern band of Washoe tribe of California-Nevada.
- 7.4 Cross Hwy. 88 to Foothill Rd.
- 8.2 Left onto Emigrant Trail.
- 11.3 Right onto Hwy. 89 (unmarked).
- 11.7 Woodfords city limits.
- 12.0 Ride ends at junction of Hwy. 88 and Hwy. 89.

Mountains and Desert

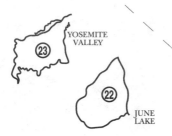

YOSEMITE
VALLEY

NEVADA

JUNE
LAKE

DEATH
VALLEY

*Pacific
Ocean*

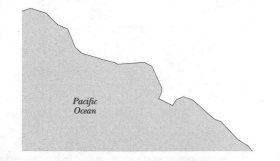

PALM
SPRINGS

Mountains and Desert

20. Death Valley Classic 114
21. Palm Springs "Triathlon" Cruise 119
22. June Lake Loop Challenge 123
23. Glacier Point Classic 127

Death Valley Classic

Furnace Creek—Bad Water—Artists Drive—
Zabriskie Point—Dante's View—Furnace Creek

It is a rough road that leads to the heights of greatness.
—Seneca, *Epistles, 84, 13*

Death Valley. The mere mention of the name conjures up images of macabre and sadomasochistic tourists making some sort of sick pilgrimage to their own diabolical mecca. Look at a map and you'll see that the National Park Service has added to the park's eerie mystique by providing ominous names for Death Valley National Monument's roadside attractions—names like Dante's View, Devil's Golf Course, and Funeral Mountains. And then there's the heat. Legend has it that on July 10, 1913, the monument was so hot that birds dropped dead in mid-flight and fell from the sky, the unwitting victims of the monument's all-time high temperature: 134 degrees.

But it's time to put these preconceived notions and tales of doom aside. Death Valley National Monument has the kind of dramatic, natural beauty that is stunning in its grandeur and, most of all, its uniqueness. From pools of pure salt to windswept sand dunes, from the lowest point in the Western Hemisphere to awe-inspiring mountaintop vistas, the monument is a rough-hewn land of earthy brilliance.

To avoid the bird-killing heat, plan your trip in the spring or fall, when temperatures are ideal for cycling. This is "tourist season" in the monument, but even so, once you get a few miles away from the Winnebagos at the Furnace Creek Visitors' Center, it's just you, your bike, and the road—with an occasional car thrown in for road-biking "reality check" purposes.

The 90-mile Death Valley Classic, which travels from 282 feet below sea level to 5,475 feet above sea level and boasts 24 consecutive uphill miles, is a doozy. Two tidbits of advice:

1. No matter how hot it is in the valley, make sure you bring a windbreaker on this ride; the nippy mountain air at the top of Dante's View will chill your sweaty body to the bone.

2. Eat a big breakfast, load your jersey pockets and fanny pack with food, and fill as many water bottles as your bike can carry. Unless you want to beg food and water from strangers at the scenic overlooks, the ride's start at Furnace Creek Ranch is the only chance you'll get to stock up—you'll find no snack bars, or even water fountains, on these lonely roads.

After a short climb from the ranch and 16 miles of downward rolling hills, you'll land at Bad Water, a small, uninspiring pond of brackish water that marks the lowest point in the Western Hemisphere, 282 feet below sea level. No doubt about it, it looks like bad water. But the glimmering fields of pure salt that extend for miles beyond to the base of distant mountains make up for Bad Water's unseemly appearance.

The road becomes twisty, narrow, and steep as you turn onto Artists Drive, a one-way tour through golden canyons laced with mineral deposits in hues of yellow, pink, and green. Then you're back on Highway 190, where the route travels uphill and south to Zabriskie Point, which overlooks the canyonlands and badlands that you just rode through. Continuing in your climbing groove, turn off for Dante's View at mile 50.7 and begin your ascent through the Black Mountains.

As the road gets steeper and steeper and the miles of climbing start to beat you down, you may begin to question whether you really care about Dante and his stupid view. Especially when you get to the ass-kicking, 14 percent grade just 0.25 mile from the top. But once you make it up there, all the pain will be forgotten in lieu of the surrounding snowcapped peaks and the dizzying views of the valley floor. Besides, all the car-driving tourists will feed your ego with a combination of disbelief, awe, and praise.

Soak in the view, reflect upon how great it is to be alive, and get ready for the big payback: 24 miles of pure and easy descending as you retrace your path back to Furnace Creek Ranch, where you'll finally be rewarded with one of life's simplest pleasures: food. Go ahead, pig out. You deserve it.

The Basics

Start: Furnace Creek Ranch, on Hwy. 190 in Death Valley National Monument.
Length: 40.8 miles or 89.5 miles.
Terrain: Long, extended climbing on quiet roads with heavy winds. Steep climbs on Artists Drive and for the last 5 miles to a mountaintop vista at Dante's View.
Food: A general store at Furnace Creek Ranch sells fruit, energy bars, and other snacks. A coffee shop next door serves breakfast, lunch, and dinner. Bring your own food and plenty of water on the ride. There are no food stops on the entire route, and only one water stop.
For more information: Death Valley National Monument, Death Valley, CA 92382; (619) 786++2331.

Miles & Directions

- 0.0 From Furnace Creek Ranch, turn right onto Hwy. 190.
- 0.9 Sea level. Turn right onto the road to Bad Water.
- 3.1 Pass Golden Canyon on your left.
- 9.6 Pass Artists Dr. on your left.
- 12.1 Pass Devil's Golf Course on your right.
- 17.7 Bad Water, 282 feet below sea level. Turnaround point. Follow road back to Artists Dr.
- 25.8 Right onto Artists Dr. Steep climb to Artist's Palette.
- 30.1 Artist's Palette vista point. Turn right for a quick look.
- 30.5 Back onto Artists Dr.
- 35.0 Right onto road to Bad Water. Head back to Hwy. 190.

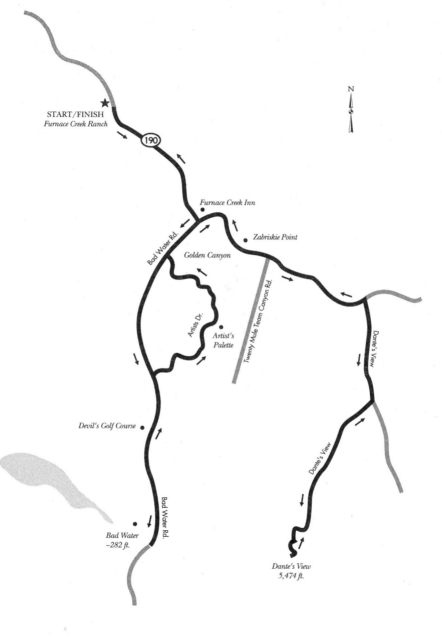

N

START/FINISH
Furnace Creek Ranch

190

Furnace Creek Inn

Zabriskie Point

Bad Water Rd.

Golden Canyon

Twenty Mule Team Canyon Rd.

Artists Dr.

Artist's Palette

Dante's View

Devil's Golf Course

Dante's View

Bad Water Rd.

Bad Water
−282 ft.

Dante's View
5,474 ft.

- 39.9 Sea level. Right onto Hwy. 190. Water, but no lunch, available at Furnace Creek Inn, across the street.

For the 40.8-mile option turn left onto Hwy. 190. Follow this road for 0.9 mile back to Furnace Creek Ranch.

- 40.0 Begin climb from sea level to 5,475 feet.
- 43.4 Zabriskie Point, 710 feet. With inspiring views of Golden Canyon, one of the most beautiful vista points in the entire park. Turn right to check out the scenic overlook.
- 44.5 Pass unpaved road: Twenty Mule Team Canyon.
- 50.7 Right onto road to Dante's View.
- 63.2 You'll be tempted, but don't drink from the water station on the side of the road. It's only for car radiators!
- 63.8 Twisty, 14 percent grade to scenic overlook at Dante's View.
- 64.2 Dante's View, 5,475 feet. Turnaround point; soar downhill all the way back to Furnace Creek Ranch!
- 77.6 Left onto Hwy. 190; back to Furnace Creek Ranch.
- 89.5 Ride ends at Furnace Creek Ranch.

21

Palm Springs "Triathlon" Cruise

Palm Springs—Mt. San Jacinto Wilderness State Park—Palm Springs

One is never entirely without the instinct of looking around.
—Walt Whitman, *Specimen Days*

So you've always wanted to try a triathlon, but you don't like to swim, and, well, you don't like to run that much either. Here's the perfect alternative triathlon. You get to combine what you like best, riding your bike, with two other cool activities. It goes like this:

Start on your bike ride with the following extra items in panniers or a backpack: (1) a bike lock; (2) comfortable clothes, including a windbreaker; (3) good walking shoes; (4) at least $14.95 in cash.

You'll ride through the parched desert terrain of sun-baked Palm Springs before hitting a turnoff for the Palm Springs Aerial Tramway at mile 3.9. Brace yourself for a strenuous climb. Sixteen percent grades characterize this road, which locals claim is one of the steepest roads in the nation. You'll wend your way from the desert floor to an elevation of 2,643 feet in approximately 4 miles. It's tough. No, it's downright grueling. But there's a reward. *(Hint: This is where your packing list comes into play.)*

After you summit the vicious climb, lock your bike. It's now time for the second leg of your triathlon. You'll need to "transi-

119

tion" into your comfy clothes and walking shoes, and you'll want to get out your $14.95.

The Palm Springs Aerial Tramway will carry you, via two eighty-passenger enclosed cars, into the San Jacinto Mountains. You'll be dropped off at 8,516 feet, where you're free to roam the 13,000-acre Mt. San Jacinto Wilderness State Park. (This is leg three of the triathlon.) With truly spectacular views and a wonderful terrain change from vast desert to vibrant wilderness, the tramway is an experience worth way more than the $15 you have to pay to get up there.

When you return to the Valley Station and are reunited with your bike, it's a breeze of a ride back down to the town, where you can eat at Congressman Sonny Bono's (yes, Cher's ex-man) restaurant, shop at the posh stores, or relax at one of the many outdoor cafes that actually pump cold air onto their patios during those unreasonably hot desert days. Thank you, Sonny! This is the life.

The Basics

Start: Palm Spring Cyclery, Palm Canyon Rd. in Palm Springs. Accessible via Hwy. 10 from Los Angeles; then connect with Rte. 111.
Length: 14.9 miles (biking only).
Terrain: One steep, grueling climb.
Food: Plenty of options in Palm Springs; also a snack bar at the tramway station.
For more information: Palm Springs Visitor Information Center, 2781 North Palm Canyon Drive, Palm Springs, CA 92258; (619) 778–8418.

Miles & Directions

- 0.0 Palm Springs Cyclery, Palm Canyon Rd. and Camino Parocela. Cross Palm Canyon Rd., then turn left onto Indian Canyon Rd.
- 3.3 Left onto San Rafael Rd.

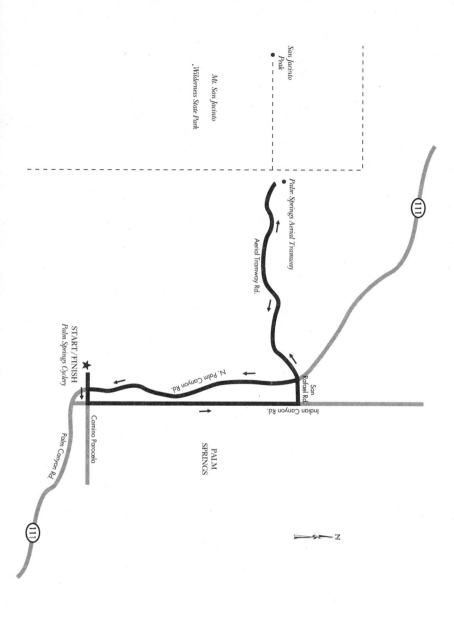

San Jacinto Peak

Mt. San Jacinto Wilderness State Park

Palm Springs Aerial Tramway

Aerial Tramway Rd.

START / FINISH
Palm Springs Cyclery

N. Palm Canyon Rd.

San Rafael Rd.

Indian Canyon Rd.

Camino Parocela

Palm Canyon Rd.

PALM SPRINGS

111

111

N

- 3.9 Cross Palm Canyon Dr.; begin steep climb to tramway.
- 7.8 Palm Springs Aerial Tramway. Lock bike at station; ascend 5,873 feet via tramway to Mt. San Jacinto Wilderness State Park.
- 7.8 After tram ride, return to bike and begin descent.
- 11.6 Veer right onto N. Palm Canyon Rd.
- 14.9 Ride ends at Palm Springs Cyclery.

22

June Lake Loop Challenge

June Lake—Silver Lake—Grant Lake—Mono Lake

> *Birth, copulation and death. Fine. In truth, however, there
> were at least two other things in which Amanda strongly be-
> lieved. Namely: magic and freedom.*
> —Tom Robbins, *Another Roadside Attraction*

Tucked away from the barren, Road Warrior-esque landscape of
Mono Lake lies a verdant and lush triad of lakes cradled by alpine
granite. Just past the desolation of Highway 395, there's an out-
cropping of summer fun waiting to be had on the June Lake Loop
Challenge. Kids on rafts, anglers with their hip boots and fishing
poles, and moms cooking up barbecues dot the shores of the ever-
inviting Silver Lake. But while the area is well used and populated
with resorts, it is not overused. Somehow the June Lake Loop has
remained a relatively quiet and composed destination. Add to that
a pristine alpine setting, inviting swimming holes, and gentle open
roads, and you've got a dreamy place where the riding is easy and
the living is good.

Traveling by two wheels is a great way to experience all this area
has to offer. And you'll find lots of good reasons to stop along the
way, be it to watch a deer leaping across the road, to cool your
sweaty body in the lake, or to check out the unreal-looking, bril-
liantly colored rock formations that rise eerily from the still water
of Mono Lake.

The ride begins at the junction of Highways 395 and 158 and
immediately climbs up the charmingly named Oh! Ridge before
dropping into the resort town of June Lake. From here the terrain

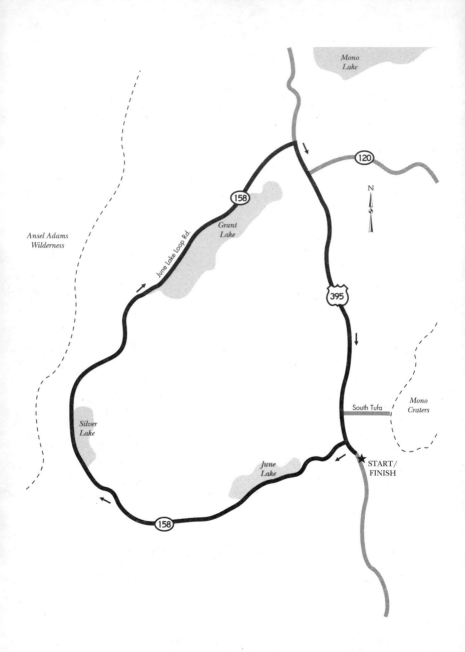

Mono Lake

120

N

Ansel Adams
Wilderness

158

Grant
Lake

June Lake Loop Rd.

395

South Tufa

Silver
Lake

Mono
Craters

June
Lake

158

★ START/
FINISH

presents few challenges as the road travels along the shores of each lake. Keep in mind, however, that the altitude never drops below 8,000 feet, so even though there aren't any major climbs, there is a good reason for that nauseated, out-of-breath, general bummer of a feeling you may be experiencing.

If you can get past altitude problems and are able to enjoy the scenery, you'll find glimmering lakes; waving, peeling birch trees; and cascading waterfalls. As you near Grant Lake, the lush scenery transforms to a desolate moonscape of jagged lake and barren hills—a foreshadowing of sights to come at Mono Lake.

After 16 miles on the tranquil June Lake Loop Challenge, you'll be faced with a decision. You can either turn around and retrace your path, or you can venture out on busy Highway 395, which isn't nearly so peaceful but does afford some cool views of the wonderfully curious Mono Lake—a sight worth beholding. And if you take Highway 395, there's even a side road (mile 16.5) you can follow out for 5 miles to check out Mono Lake's South Tufa.

Either way, you can't go wrong—these 22 or 32 miles combine some of the best elements of bike riding into one neat package— the luxury of beautiful terrain; the freedom of gentle, less traveled roads; the magic of mind-expanding sights; and the satisfaction of a good workout.

The Basics

Start: June Lake Loop Rd., southern end, at intersection of Hwy. 395 and Hwy. 158.
Length: 22 or 32 miles.
Terrain: Rolling hills to flat. Less traffic on Hwy. 158; more traffic on Hwy. 395. Not advisable in winter months.
Food: There's a general store at the ride start, plus restaurants and stores, mostly situated in June Lake, as you travel around the loop.
For more information: Mammoth Lakes Ranger Station, P.O. Box 148, Mammoth Lake, CA 93546; (619) 934–2505.

Miles & Directions

- 0.0 June Lake Loop Rd., southern end, at intersection of Hwy. 395 and Hwy. 158; take Hwy. 158 (June Lake Loop Rd.).
- 0.7 Begin climb.
- 1.1 Oh! Ridge.
- 2.4 June Lake city limits.
- 6.5 Silver Lake.
- 11.1 Grant Lake.
- 15.0 Mono Craters.
- 16.0 Hwy. 158 intersects with Hwy. 395; right onto Hwy. 395.

Option: You can turn around at the intersection and retrace your path on the less traveled June Lake Loop Rd. for a total of 32 miles.

- 16.5 Mono Lake, South Tufa turnoff option (will add 10 miles to total).
- 22.2 Ride ends at intersection of Hwy. 395 and Hwy. 158.

23

Glacier Point Classic

Yosemite Valley—Chiquapin—
Glacier Point—Yosemite Valley

Yosemite Valley, to me, is always a sunrise, a glitter of green
and golden wonder in a vast edifice of stone and space.
—Ansel Adams, *The Portfolios of Ansel Adams*

If ever there was a climb that was worth the agony, it is the excruciating and unyielding grind up to Glacier Point, which rests high above the Yosemite Valley. Atop Glacier Point the halting views of Half Dome and Yosemite Falls seem like a miracle, and all the possibilities of the world become magically apparent. When your knees start quivering at the Glacier Point vista area, it won't be the 25 miles of climbing that's causing you to shake in your cleats—it'll be the striking, mystical, tear-evoking view.

Your road to nirvana begins in the hub of Yosemite Valley mayhem, where tourists from every corner of the globe clamber through aisles of souvenir T-shirts, visors, and snow domes. Most of these people will never make it past the crammed campgrounds and snack bars of the valley, and as with any road to enlightenment, the steps (or pedalstrokes) you take away from the masses are the ones that mark your pathway to greatness. It seems like the tougher the journey, the greater the rewards.

And so your route winds out of the valley and begins the harrowing, daunting climb to Glacier Point. Be forewarned: In order to endure this ride, you've got to have a bit of sadomasochism in your blood. It's just that hard. Another info-nugget: No matter how hot it is in the valley, bring a windbreaker. You'll be traveling from the valley floor to 7,214 feet.

At mile 8.3 you get your first glimpse of views to come and also an opportune excuse to stretch your legs when you reach the Tunnel View, where the valley and its surrounding mountains lie before you in all their glory. Forge ahead for another 8 miles and you'll reach Chiquapin, a town that doesn't seem to have a population but does at least have a store where you can take a break and load up on snacks and whatnot. From here you've got another 14 uphill miles through alpine birch and past huge slabs of granite en route to the granddaddy of all granite formations: Half Dome.

Two miles from the vista area, you'll summit the climb and be treated to a steep and winding descent. Then, at mile 32.3, you can finally dismount your bike, wobble off to a bench on your noodley legs, and soak up the natural wonders of Yosemite—an experience heightened by rushing, pumping endorphins. And when you finally get to the top, dripping and exhausted, you can say "ha!" to all the car drivers up there. They think you're a maniac, they think you're sick—but you know better. You know what they're missing.

The Basics

Start: Yosemite Valley Visitor Center in Yosemite Village, accessible via Hwy. 120 or Hwy. 140.

Length: 64.8 miles.

Terrain: Steep, extended mountain climbing; some high-traffic areas; most advisable on weekdays in the fall or spring. Road closed in winter.

Food: Stock up on food-on-the-fly at the Yosemite Village grocery store. There's a store in Chiquapin that might be open, but other than that you're on your own. Bring as much water as you can possibly carry. This is a ride on which you need to be completely self-sufficient.

For more information: Park Information Service, P.O. Box 577, Yosemite National Park, Yosemite, CA 95389; (209) 372–0265.

N

START/FINISH
Valley Visitor Center

• *Half Dome*

Main Rd.

Yosemite

Main Rd.

• *Glacier Point*

El Capitan

Valley

• *Tunnel View*

41

Glacier Point Rd.

Chiquapin Rd.

CHIQUAPIN

Miles & Directions

- 0.0 Valley Visitor Center; follow signs TOWARD PARK EXIT.
- 0.3 Veer right onto Main Rd.
- 5.7 Left onto Hwy. 41; begin climb.
- 6.7 Right onto Hwy. 41 to Glacier Point.
- 8.3 Tunnel View.
- 16.2 Left onto Chiquapin Rd. (becomes Glacier Point Rd.).
- 30.3 Begin steep descent!
- 32.3 Half Dome and Glacier Point; turn around and retrace path back to Yosemite Valley.
- 64.8 Ride ends at Valley Visitor Center.

Southern California

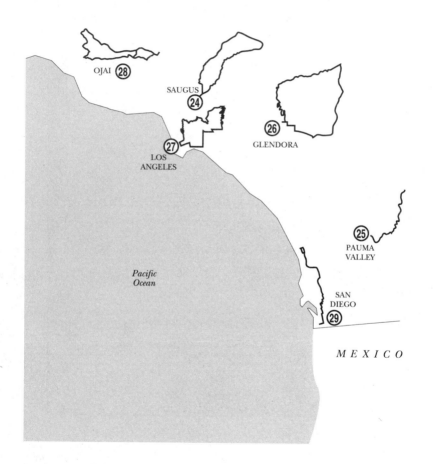

OJAI (28)

SAUGUS
(24)

GLENDORA
(26)

LOS
ANGELES
(27)

PAUMA
VALLEY
(25)

Pacific
Ocean

SAN
DIEGO
(29)

MEXICO

Southern California

24. Canyon Country Challenge 134
25. Mt. Palomar Challenge 139
26. Mt. Baldy Challenge 143
27. Los Angeles Urban Cruise 148
28. Ojai Ramble 153
29. Torrey Pines Ramble 157

24

Canyon Country Challenge

Saugus—Los Angeles Aqueduct—Green Valley—
Leona Valley—San Andreas Fault—
Bouquet Reservoir—Saugus

Flee as a bird to your mountain.
—Psalms, 11:1

It's a cyclist's nightmare. A maze of flat colors, stoplights, strip malls, and big hair has you trapped and confused like a lab rat facing its final hour. Bitter motorists with Big Gulps in hand are flipping you the bird as their cars upchuck exhaust right in your bike-riding path. Light rock oozes in your ears. You want out desperately. You suddenly feel as if you can't breathe. Frantically, you look around for something—anything—that's pure. But gas stations and tract homes clog your view for as far as the eye can see. What to do? Where to go?

If these feelings of anxiety plague you as you roll into the Canyon Country Challenge's ride start in Saugus, fear not, fellow nature lover. The San Fernando Valley can indeed be a scary place, but a surprisingly large amount of open space has escaped the evil developer's hand. And intrepid bicyclists who choose to ride here will find that the bucolic canyons rising majestically from the rubble of this suburban wasteland provide some of the best rural riding in all of Los Angeles County.

The transformation begins with the start of Sanfrancisquito Canyon Road at mile 2.4. This quiet, less traveled backroad is tucked between clay-colored canyon walls dotted with scrubby green brush, while the taller peaks of the Angeles National Forest paint the distance with their steep, sloping contours. The route remains basically flat until you pass a fire station at mile 8.9, where you'll be treated to a far-out vision of the Los Angeles Aqueduct stretching over a hill in three giant, fleshy tentacles of peach-colored piping.

Beyond the gargantuan pipes the road begins to rise, and the canyon walls close in a bit more. As you begin climbing, Dr. Seuss vegetation juts wildly from earthy rocks. Spiky, angly bushes grow from the tiniest canyon cracks, and spindly plants with poofy white flowers at their tops stand stoically askew, bearing an amazing resemblance to giant toilet-bowl scrubbers. It's like riding through a psychedelic cartoon produced by Nature.

Watching the vegetation is a good diversion from the serious climbing you'll be undertaking. For nearly 13 miles, you'll be spinning (or maybe grinding) uphill on this road. At mile 19.5, when you'll probably be feeling anything but spunky, you hit Spunky Canyon Road, where you'll have a chance to take a break and get some food. There's a little community up here complete with a general store. To reach it, turn in on Spunky Canyon Road and pedal for about 1 mile. You can also cut the ride short by taking Spunky Canyon to Bouquet Canyon Road and turning right. This'll save you about 15 miles of pedaling, but you'll also miss the joy of summiting Sanfrancisquito Road, as well as a lot of cool riding in the Leona Valley.

When you reach the top of Sanfrancisquito, the road opens up to grassy, lumpy fields where a lone windmill spins quietly and methodically in the soft rush of the breeze. A dilapidated building that may once have been a gas station stands deserted and crumbling on the side of the road, a victim of the persistent organic matter steadily overtaking its structure. And since there are virtually no automobiles up here, it's easy to understand why this business venture failed.

You are now in the Leona Valley, and as you turn onto Elizabeth Lake Road and ride along the spine of the canyon, you'll be riding right on top of the San Andreas Fault line. Ranches spread out on countless acres of land, and livestock graze freely in the multitude of open space. This small community of farm homes is loosely tied together by the Rancher's Market at mile 28.2, and you'll be surprised to find that there's even a Mexican restaurant up here.

When you get to Bouquet Canyon Road, you'll be faced with more tough climbing. You won't be home free until you see the Bouquet Reservoir at mile 36.6. This reservoir, which abruptly appears over the crest of your final climb, is a strikingly pretty man-made lake that serves as part of the Los Angeles water system. Twisting below the canyon walls, this small lake immediately looks too funky to be natural, yet it fits in perfectly with the Dr. Seuss plants and the giant tentacle pipes of the aqueduct. Little islands of vegetation spring from the water to complete the reservoir's lovely picture, and even in its unnatural state, it forms quite a vision of grandeur.

A dam nixes the lake as quickly as it appeared, and from here the all-out descending begins. The terrain gets thicker—even lush—as you drop for 10 miles through the Angeles National Forest. After 50 miles of riding, you're back in Santa Clarita, where you'll have a 3.5-mile ride back to Saugus. As you finish cycling and peel yourself off your bike, think for a moment about the miles you've traveled. Suburb total: 6. Rural total: 47. This is what they call an exodus; this is getting away from it all. And this is what it's all about.

The Basics

Start: Newhall Ranch Rd. and Bouquet Canyon Rd. in Saugus. Take I–5 north from Los Angeles to the Valencia Blvd. exit. Take Valencia Blvd. east to Bouquet Canyon Rd. Turn left onto Bouquet Canyon Rd. and proceed to Newhall Ranch Rd.

Length: 53.5 miles.

Terrain: Extended climbing on quiet country roads. Heavy traffic for 4 miles from Santa Clarita to Saugus.

Food: Hughes Market at the ride's start in Saugus, as well as a variety of fast-food emporiums. General store on Spunky Canyon Rd. (mile 19.5), and another store, the Rancher's Market, at mile 28.2.

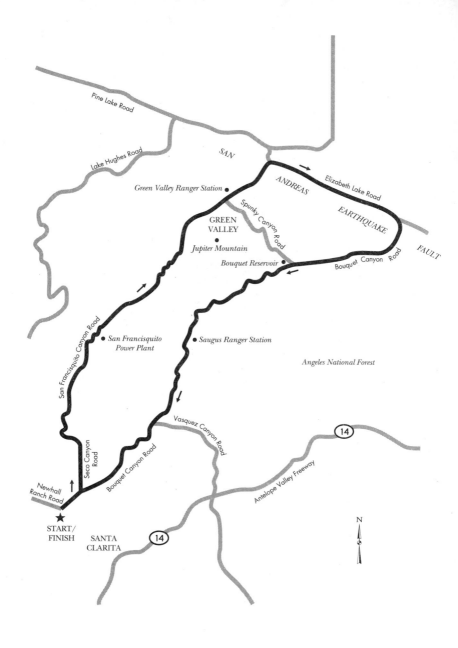

For More Information: San Fernando Valley Bicycle Club, P.O. Box 4053, Chatsworth, CA, 91313; (818) 787–2788.

Miles & Directions

- 0.0 At the intersection of Bouquet Canyon Rd. and Newhall Ranch Rd., turn right (north) onto Bouquet Canyon.
- 0.5 Left onto Seco Canyon Rd.
- 2.4 Seco Canyon Rd. becomes Sanfrancisquito Canyon Rd.
- 6.4 Enter Angeles National Forest.
- 8.9 Fire station; begin climbing.
- 19.5 Stop sign at Spunky Canyon Rd.; continue straight. For food and drink, turn right on Spunky Canyon and continue for 1 mile to the general store in Green Valley.
- 21.0 Green Valley Ranger Station.
- 21.8 Summit.
- 22.6 Right onto Elizabeth Lake Rd.
- 29.4 Right onto Bouquet Canyon Rd.
- 36.6 Bouquet Reservoir.
- 45.5 Saugus Ranger Station.
- 46.0 Leave Angeles National Forest.
- 49.7 Santa Clarita city limits.
- 53.5 Left onto Newhall Ranch Rd.; ride ends.

25

Mt. Palomar Challenge

Pauma Valley—Palomar Mountain—
Mt. Palomar Observatory—Pauma Valley

Climb every mountain.
> —Julie Andrews, *The Sound of Music*

It's reputed to be one of the toughest climbs in America. It's been known to break some of the most hardy world-class cyclists and triathletes. Even the mention of its name evokes fear in the heart of many an intrepid rider.

The unrelenting Mt. Palomar has earned itself a dubious reputation in the cycling community. So why would you want to attempt it? Probably for the same reason that so many other cyclists suffer up its steep slopes: Because it's there.

At 5,256 feet, it may not come close to being the highest peak in California, but its road to the top is up there among the steepest. The ride starts in the Pauma Valley and twists through miles of orange groves that often leave a rolling carpet of citrus covering the ground. As the climbing begins, all rows or forms of planned vegetation give way to wild, random indigenous plants, including tall pines that shade your ascent and form lacy shadow patterns on the asphalt. These are the things that grab your attention and stick in your mind when you're trying not to dwell on the pain of this steep climb.

After nearly 13 miles of climbing, you'll get a break when you reach East Grade Road and the Palomar Mountain General Store and Restaurant. Here you'll find everything you need to make it to the Mt. Palomar Observatory, which rests at the tippy-top of the peak.

From the store a nice reprieve from climbing awaits. After dropping for a few miles through the piney woods, you'll be back to the grind as you traverse upward for another 2.4 miles to the observatory. The climbing's easier here, partly because of the gentler grade and partly because you know how close you are.

Mt. Palomar Observatory is a groovy sideshow that's well worth the climb. It houses one of the largest telescopes in the world, the Hale telescope, which has an incomprehensible range of one billion light-years. The photographs it takes of the galaxy are on display at the observatory, but even more interesting is the way everything is presented. The observatory hasn't updated its presentation materials much since the 1950s, and entering the structure is like being privy to a major time warp. Even the postcards in the gift shop are dated, featuring Technicolor snapshots of clean-cut scientists in chartreuse-colored shirts and wing tips.

All of this presents a great opportunity to stretch your legs and prepare for the big payback: nearly 18 miles of ease and exhilaration as you coast down Mt. Palomar and get a clearer perspective on how steep those grades really were.

The Basics

Start: Hwy. 76, at Pauma Village; accessible via Hwy. 15 from San Diego.

Length: 36.2 miles.

Terrain: Steep mountain climbing; heavy traffic in some spots (most advisable on weekdays).

Food: There's a general store in Pauma Village at the ride start, but there's nothing else until you reach the Palomar Mountain General Store and Restaurant at mile 13.2.

For more information: San Diego County Bicycle Coalition, P.O. Box 34544, San Diego, CA 92163; (619) 294–4916.

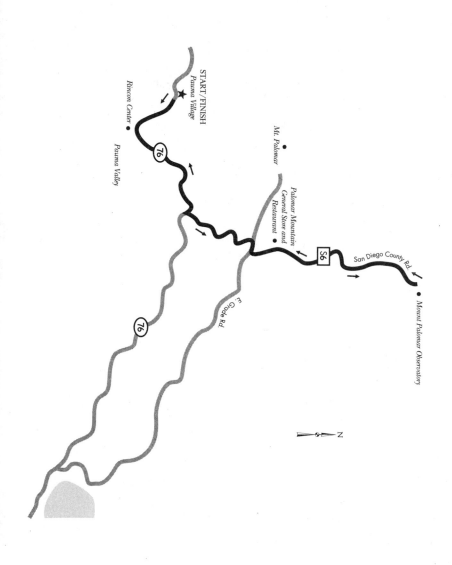

START/FINISH
Pauma Village

Rincon Center

Pauma Valley

76

76

E. Grade Rd.

Mt. Palomar

Palomar Mountain
General Store and
Restaurant

S6

San Diego County Rd

Mount Palomar Observatory

N

Miles & Directions

- 0.0 From Pauma Village on Hwy. 76, go east on Hwy. 76 toward Mt. Palomar.
- 1.6 Rincon Center. Follow Hwy. 76, which curves toward Mt. Palomar; begin climbing.
- 6.6 Left onto San Diego County Rd. S6 toward Mt. Palomar.
- 13.2 Left onto E. Grade Rd., following S6. Palomar Mountain General Store and Restaurant; begin descent.
- 15.4 More climbing to observatory.
- 17.8 S6 ends; follow path to observatory.
- 18.1 Mt. Palomar Observatory. Turnaround point; retrace your path back to Pauma Village.
- 36.2 Ride ends at Pauma Village.

26

Mt. Baldy Challenge

Glendora—Angeles National Forest—
Baldy Village—Claremont—Glendora

> *I went to the woods because I wished to live deliberately, to*
> *front only the essential facts of life, and see if I could not*
> *learn what it had to teach, and not, when I came to die, dis-*
> *cover that I had not lived.*
> —Henry David Thoreau, *Walden* II, What I Lived For

What could possibly be more life-affirming than climbing a mountain—than straddling your bicycle, pushing off a sunny, suburban sidewalk, and heading for the proverbial hills?

While it's not exactly easy to find a suburb that boasts mountains in its backyard, the Los Angeles 'burb of Glendora is precisely such a place. From this ride's start at Sierra Madre and Glendora Mountain roads, you can almost taste the deliciously clean mountain air swelling just a few miles above. Within minutes of taking to the road, you are spinning high above Glendora, floating in the rare bliss of freedom that sometimes occurs when a ride is just right: when you're traveling on a carless road, and traversing a huge hunk of uncivilized land.

Within 0.5 mile of your Glendora start, you'll enter the Angeles National Forest, where you'll leave houses—and all other worries of civilized life—behind you. As you wend your way up Glendora Mountain Road's endless succession of switchbacks, you are engulfed in a rich texture of rocky foothills and lush forestland. Wildflowers spill from the edges of the road onto your path, and the landscape is fertile and inviting, urging you to continue upward toward the distant snowy peaks. Far off the side of the mountain, the city of Glendora glistens demurely, with only a hint of its fast-paced, hurry-scurry lifestyle apparent from atop your peaceful mountain vista.

But all the natural beauty in the world can't disguise the fact that you'll face 20 miles of climbing before you reach a summit. And that much climbing is hard on the ole legs and lungs. Thin mountain air doesn't help. Take your time, and make the most of this incredibly rewarding climb. Stop often to smell the flowers and take in the views. Go on and do it. You'll thank me later.

As you continue your ascent into the mountains, mammoth peaks overtake the foreground, rising straight ahead on your bike-riding path. The only sounds now are the rhythmic swish of your cadence and perhaps the heavy flapping of wings, as hungry hawks hover above, hunting for the mice that will be their dinner. Any traces of urbanization are gone. You have penetrated the wilds of nature, and from here to Baldy Village, it's just you and your bike against the challenges of terrain, random weather (be prepared for anything), and whatever else Nature decides to throw at you.

After 21 miles of climbing, you'll get your just desserts as you jam down into Baldy Village, where you'll find a water hose (hidden in the planter at the fire station), a restaurant, and a little store. After all the miles of seclusion, Baldy Village is like a mountain mirage, appearing out of nowhere and pleasantly surprising you with its offerings.

From here you'll get to enjoy a fast descent on Mt. Baldy Road, which is much less secluded than Glendora Mountain Road but is still great for the purposes of free and easy downhilling. When you eventually drop back into the heavily populated suburb of Claremont, you'll have 10 miles of riding in traffic before you reach Glendora.

This gives you plenty of time to ponder the mysteries of life. Imagine having all this nature as your backyard playground. Kinda makes you wonder why Glendora Mountain Road isn't jammed with carloads of fun-seeking suburbanites wishing to commune with nature. Have they yet to discover the drama of these ridges?

The glory of their seclusion? Mustn't these jagged mountain roads with their fresh, crisp air be more life-affirming than the exhaust-laden highways that lead to jam-packed restaurants and such? Why can so few people see the value of pushing limits, reaching new heights? Certainly, this is one of life's mysteries. But as you think about it, just be glad that you know the truth. And pray that the masses don't get enlightened anytime soon.

The Basics

Start: Sierra Madre and Glendora Mtn. Rd., Glendora, northern Los Angeles County.
Length: 42 miles.
Terrain: Steep mountain climbing; swift, tricky descending. From Glendora to Baldy Village, cars are not an issue; traffic picks up after Baldy Village.
Food: Many chain restaurants and grocery stores in Glendora. Stock up on food and water for the ride; you won't have any options until you reach Baldy Village at mile 22.3, where there's a water hose, a general store, and a restaurant.
For more information: Claremont College Cycling Team, Bud's Bike Shop, 217 W. 1st St., Claremont, CA 91711; (909) 621–5827.

Miles & Directions

- 0.0 Sierra Madre and Glendora Mtn. Rd. Heading north on Glendora Mtn. Rd., begin climbing.
- 0.5 Dalton Ranger Station, Angeles National Forest.
- 9.9 Veer right off main road toward Baldy Village.
- 21.2 Begin descent into Baldy Village.
- 22.1 Baldy Village. Left onto Mt. Baldy Rd.
- 22.3 Mt. Baldy Lodge Restaurant and Store. Turnaround point; begin descent of Mt. Baldy Rd.
- 27.9 Leave Angeles National Forest; enter Claremont.
- 30.6 Veer left at Mills.

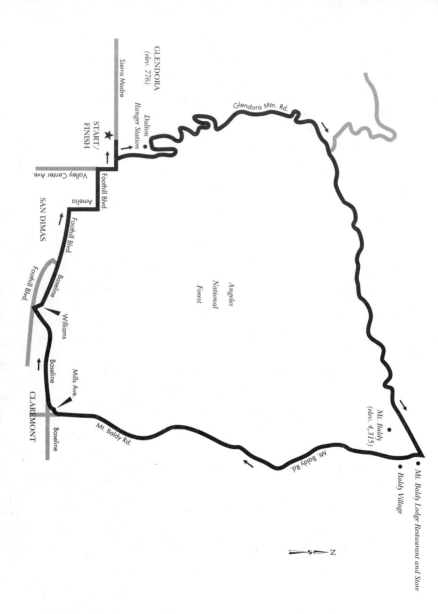

- 31.8 Right onto Baseline.
- 35.4 Right at T onto Williams.
- 35.5 Left at stop sign; road becomes Baseline again.
- 37.7 Right onto Foothill Blvd.
- 39.0 Glendora city limits.
- 39.5 Right onto Amelia.
- 40.4 Left onto Foothill Blvd.
- 41.2 Right onto Valley Center at Glendora High School.
- 41.9 Valley Center becomes Sierra Madre.
- 42.0 Ride ends at Sierra Madre and Glendora Mtn. Rd.

27

Los Angeles Urban Cruise

Griffith Park—Mulholland Drive—Beverly Hills—
Hollywood—Griffith Park

> *A city has values as well as slums, excitement as well as*
> *conflict . . . a personality that has not yet been obliterated*
> *by its highways and gas stations.*
> —Charles Abrams, *The City Is the Frontier*

No city is looked upon with as much disdain by outsiders as the poor, battered city of Los Angeles. On top of its bad reputation, which has spanned the decades, the city has been through fires, riots, and earthquakes in the past few years. Let's face it: This joint has been through the ringer. But as war-torn and ravaged as it may be, as cheesy, glitzy, and phony as it has been depicted, Los Angeles is still the City of Angels, and even with its scars and pockmarks—or perhaps because of them—it has a certain crooked charm that is undeniable.

Your urban adventure through the ever-changing streets of Los Angeles starts at Griffith Park and heads immediately for a brisk climb up Mulholland Drive. If the name of this famous hilltop road isn't familiar to you, think back to all the romantic movie scenes where the boy drives the girl to the vista point above Los Angeles. Arms intertwined, they stare dreamily at the twinkling lights of the city below. This is Mulholland Drive. The place where Marilyn Monroe reputedly lost her virginity. The place where today's teenagers still come to make out and party. During the day these types of shenanigans aren't going on, but you still get astounding views of a frantic and vital city sprawling below.

As you roll along on hilly Mulholland Drive past cacti and palm-treed front lawns, as well as houses perched precariously on stilts along the side of the mountain, views of the Pacific Ocean and the never-ending stretch of city alternate from side to side. At mile 13 the climbing ends, and you're treated to a fast descent down Benedict Canyon Drive, which takes you from six-pack-toting teenage turf to the champagne-and-limo territory of Beverly Hills.

You'll know you've arrived in the hills of Beverly when the grass magically turns from a dull, seaweed color to a cartoonlike Technicolor green. Potted plants line the sidewalks, and circular driveways flaunt Ferraris and Jags.

Your route takes a quick side trip to the cutest (yes, cutest) house in all of Beverly Hills. On the corner of Walden Drive and Carmelita Avenue, you'll find what's known in these parts as the Witch's House. You can't miss it. Straight out of *Grimm's Fairy Tales*, it's a crooked, shingled house whose yard is delightfully overgrown with wildflowers. The house's history includes use in the 1920s as the set for a silent version of *Hansel and Gretel*.

From here, you'll navigate jam-packed Rodeo Drive—another oft-filmed Los Angeles spot, this one boasting all kinds of fancy stores that probably don't admit sweaty cyclists inside their stuffy doors. From here it's just a hop, skip, and jump to the Sunset Strip, and you're on your way to Hollywood.

Turning onto Hollywood Boulevard at mile 25.8 steers you right into the garish, touristy, and seedy (therefore fun and spine-tingling) underbelly of Los Angeles. You can see things like the Chinese Theatre, where all the stars have pressed their feet in the cement; the Max Factor Beauty Museum, where you can learn how the movie stars are made up; and the headquarters for Frederick's of Hollywood, where you can see the panties of the stars (no kidding!). But since leaving your bike outside may not be a good idea on Hollywood Boulevard, seeing it all in a blur of colors and lights is a good option. Besides, by going inside any of these tempting emporiums of garishness, you run the risk of becoming jaded by discovering that what masquerades as glamorous glitz is just another tourist trap.

Best to head on to Griffith Park, arguably the best part of the entire ride. After you've battled the urban warriors for 28 miles, Griffith Park offers a welcome oasis amid the chaotic city. Narrow roads wind up the park's rather intimidating hill, which leads to the Griffith Park Observatory. As you wend your way up this tough climb, look for squirrels, and even an occasional deer, darting into thick bushes off the side of the road. Lest you forget, amid all this natural beauty, that you're in Los Angeles, there's a bust of James Dean at the top of Griffith Park where the observatory is perched. The observatory, which was used to film scenes from Dean's *Rebel without a Cause,* offers more great views of the Los Angeles area, including a splendid vista of the famed Hollywood sign.

In fact, you'll get to ride even closer to that sign as you make your way back to Travel Town via a beautifully quiet climb (followed by a long descent) on Mt. Hollywood Drive. At the end of your descent, you're virtually back to Travel Town, where you can reflect back on your journey and think of all you took in on this 36-mile tour.

The Basics

Start: Travel Town in Griffith Park, Los Angeles.
Length: 36 miles.
Terrain: Busy city streets, narrow shoulders at times, some steep climbing, varying road conditions.
Food: Options galore! A few miles on Mulholland Dr. and in Griffith Park are the only places where food of some sort isn't readily available.
For more information: Los Angeles Wheelmen, P.O. Box 3432, City of Industry, CA 91744; (213) 661–0070. Or The Los Angeles Visitor and Convention Bureau, Hilton Hotel, 685 South Figueroa Street, Los Angeles CA 90017; (213) 689–8822.

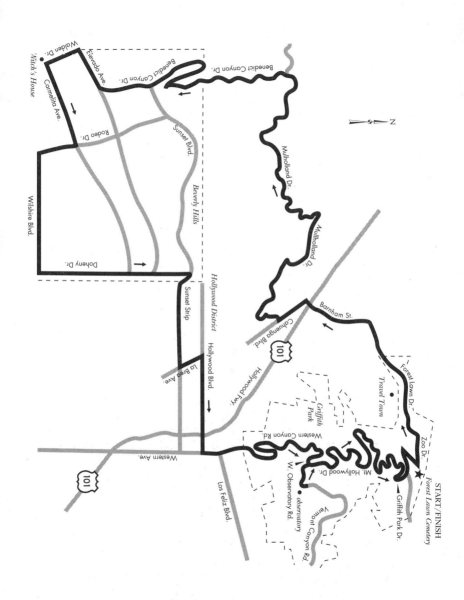

Miles & Directions

- 0.0 From Travel Town go straight onto Zoo Dr., heading out of the park.
- 0.2 Left onto Forest Lawn Dr.
- 1.2 Forest Lawn Cemetery.
- 2.2 Left onto Barnham St.
- 3.1 Cross Hwy. 101.
- 3.3 Left onto Cahuenga Blvd.
- 3.8 Left onto Mulholland Dr.; begin steep climb.
- 4.6 Vista/make-out point.
- 5.4 Summit.
- 7.9 Stoplight at Laurel Canyon Dr.; continue straight.
- 10.7 Veer left, staying on Mullholland Dr.
- 13.0 Left onto Benedict Canyon Dr.
- 17.1 Beverly Hills.
- 18.5 Right onto Elevado Ave.
- 19.2 Left onto Walden Dr.
- 19.3 Left onto Carmelita Ave. Witch's House.
- 19.7 Right onto Rodeo Dr.
- 20.4 Left onto Wilshire Blvd.
- 21.0 Left onto Doheny Dr.
- 22.7 Right onto Sunset Strip.
- 25.5 Left onto La Brea Ave.
- 25.8 Right onto Hollywood Blvd.
- 27.4 Cross Hollywood Fwy.
- 28.0 Left onto Western Ave.; begin climb.
- 28.4 Left at Griffith Park entrance (Western Canyon Rd.).
- 30.4 Right onto W. Observatory Rd.
- 31.0 Summit at observatory. Turnaround point; head back down Western Canyon Rd.
- 31.3 Left at stop sign (Mt. Hollywood Dr.). Follow sign TO TRAVEL TOWN; if gate is closed, go around it. Begin 1-mile climb.
- 32.8 Veer left, following Mt. Hollywood Dr. to Travel Town.
- 35.3 Left onto Griffith Park Dr.
- 36.0 Ride ends at Travel Town.

28

Ojai Ramble

A bicycle does get you there and more.... And there is always the thin edge of danger to keep you alert and comfortably apprehensive. Dogs become dogs again and snap at your raincoat; potholes become personal. And getting there is all the fun.

—Bill Emerson, *Saturday Evening Post*

Less than 100 miles away from the excess of Los Angeles, a skinny inchworm of a road undulates through quiet Southern California countryside as it elegantly and decidedly makes its urban exodus. Curling over hills and stretching through farmland, this asphalt leads lazily to the lost little community of Ojai.

As it turns out, the twisty-turny roads leading to Ojai are some of the best reasons to visit, and cyclists from all over Southern California flock to the Ojai Valley on a regular basis to flit about on its curvy backroads. The city itself is neither vital enough to be particularly intriguing nor small enough to be charmingly rural, but its uncrowded beauty and open space render it a pampering and bucolic retreat from the typical Southern California lifestyle—and that is what has made it special. Unlike most of its neighboring areas, it's a place that hasn't been washed away by the sterile signposts of suburbia. Tract homes and factory outlets have not found their way here. Instead, a soft outline of mountains, shade from arching oak trees, endless rows of native orange groves, and myriad horse ranches are the area's defining factors. And in Ojai getting away from it all is as easy as rolling off the main drag in any direction atop your two-wheeled companion.

The Ojaians are especially proud of their extensive bike path. It provides a flat and predictable route, with no sharp turns, that starts in downtown Ojai and extends for 9 miles. It's a fabulous family bike ride and an awfully nice path, but being that it's so safe and certain, it's not the stuff a real bike tour's made of. Your route inevitably turns off it after 1.8 miles and rolls toward the real cycling heartland.

The adventure starts on Creek Road, which gyrates its way across the floor of the Ojai Valley. Tree-covered hills cup the road and provide lush vistas from every imaginable angle. Around each new bend sinewy horses graze on a verdant carpet of grass and gallop through the open fields of the ranches they live on. All along the way a gentle creek follows faithfully at your side, whispering its soft, rumbling song for you, the horses, or any other astute listener to hear.

But this brook babble abruptly becomes craggy chaos as you are shocked into the reality of cars on Highway 33. **Be careful.** By this point Creek Road has lulled you into a drooling stupor, and now Highway 33 will be demanding all your wits and your sharpest attention. It's a trafficky stretch, but you've got to endure it only for 1 mile before you tumble back into nature on Santa Ana Boulevard.

The next challenge comes in the form of a 1-mile climb to Lake Casitas. This mild-mannered hill is the only extended climb on the ride, so depending upon your mindset, you can hammer it, savor it, or just plain endure it. When you get to the top, 2,700-acre Lake Casitas magically appears before your eyes, and from here you'll enjoy excellent vistas of the entire Lake Casitas Recreation Area as you cruise high above the lake's tree-lined shores. And as you get closer to the lake, you'll discover that some of these trees aren't of the typical lakeside variety: They're palm trees.

As you leave Lake Casitas, Highway 150 wends past orange groves and skips over the Ventura River before catching up with the bike path that'll lead you back to Ojai. About 0.5 mile before hitting the bike path, you'll pass the stately Krotona Institute, a widely recognized spiritual center housing a library of more than 10,000 books on religion, philosophy, and theosophy. From here hook up with the bike path and spin your legs out for the next 2 miles as you pedal back to Ojai Avenue, where *chili rellenos* and *cerveza* await.

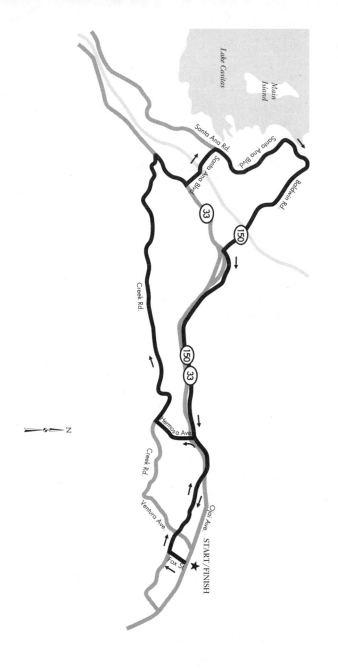

The Basics

Start: Ojai Ave. (Hwy. 150) and Fox St. in downtown Ojai.
Length: 18.1 miles.
Terrain: Mostly flat, with a 1-mile climb; rural roads, with 1 mile of heavy traffic on Hwy. 33.
Food: Myriad Mexican restaurants in downtown Ojai; there's also a big grocery store, Von's, at "the Y" (mile 1.4 on your route).
For more information: Oxnard/Ventura Bicycle Club; (805) 650–1794.

Miles & Directions

- 0.0 Ojai Ave. and Fox St.; turn onto Fox St.
- 0.2 Right onto bike path at Ojai Valley Racquet Club.
- 1.4 Bike path ends at "the Y"; cross Ventura Ave. and turn left onto Ventura at the strip mall and onto the bike path.
- 1.8 Left onto Hermosa Ave.
- 2.5 Right onto Creek Rd.
- 6.8 Right onto Hwy. 33. **Caution:** Heavy traffic.
- 7.9 Left onto Santa Ana Blvd. (called Ojai Dr. on the other side of street), following the sign TO LAKE CASITAS.
- 8.8 Right onto Santa Ana Rd.
- 9.0 Begin climb.
- 9.7 Lake Casitas.
- 10.0 Summit.
- 11.4 Lake Casitas Recreation Area.
- 11.5 Right onto Hwy. 150 (Baldwin Rd.).
- 13.8 Cross bridge at Ventura River.
- 14.7 Left onto bike path at Ventura Ave.
- 16.2 Krotona Institute.
- 16.7 Veer right at "the Y" onto bike path.
- 17.9 Left onto Fox St.
- 18.1 Ride ends at Fox St. and Ojai Ave.

29

Torrey Pines Ramble

*La Jolla Shores—University of California at
San Diego—Del Mar—Torrey Pines State Reserve—
La Jolla Shores*

> *Far out in the ocean the water is as blue as the petals of the
> loveliest cornflower and as clear as the purest glass.*
> —Hans Christian Andersen,
> *Fairy Tales, The Little Mermaid*

Behind the all-too-real stereotypes of bleached-blond hair and
skintight neon outfits, and amid a populace of nearly three million, there still lies the beautifully pure coast and near-perfect
weather of San Diego, which, in many ways, comes just about as
close to paradise as you can get.

The Torrey Pines Ramble is a carefree tour of some of the most
beautiful scenery San Diego has to offer—and you barely have to
leave the city to see it. The ride starts at La Jolla Shores Beach,
which on a nice day (nearly every day in San Diego is nice) is jam-
packed with sun worshipers.

Almost immediately after starting this ride you're faced with a
major climb that snakes up La Jolla Shores Drive to UC San Diego.
From here the route drops down to cruise along the Pacific Ocean,
which curves into the distance just like a landscape you would expect to see in the south of France.

As you coast along the ocean, Torrey Pines Road becomes
Camino Del Mar as you near the posh and ultraluxe seaside town
of Del Mar. When you pedal into town, take Fifteenth Street down

to the train station and beach, where the glaringly green grass and abnormally blue skies that usually prevail make you feel like you're pedaling in a touched-up postcard. It just seems too brilliant to be real.

Soak up the atmosphere for a while before mounting your bike and heading back toward La Jolla. At mile 12.6 turn into the Torrey Pines State Reserve, where you'll climb up a steep, car-free road that twists elegantly through the park's exotic foliage and its namesake Torrey Pines. From the top you'll be rewarded with spectacular views of the La Jolla beaches. Count your blessings if you're able to time this ride to arrive at the top of Torrey Pines at sunset. It's a truly awe-inspiring view.

From here you'll have a quick descent down La Jolla Shores Drive, and then you're back to the tanning-crazed beach, where you can plunk down on the sand and join the masses or visit the Scripps Institute of Oceanography, which houses more than twenty tanks of vibrantly colored saltwater fish.

The Basics

Start: La Jolla Shores Beach; accessible via Hwy. 274 to La Jolla Shores Blvd.
Length: 17.6 miles.
Terrain: Hilly; some extended climbing; some busy roads.
Food: This is a relatively urban ride, so food options are everywhere, but your best bet is Del Mar.
For more information: International Visitor Information Center, 11 Horton Plaza, San Diego, CA 92101; (619) 236–1212. San Diego County Bicycle Coalition, P.O. Box 34544, San Diego, CA 92163; (619) 294–4916.

Miles & Directions

■ 0.0 Camino Del Oro and Frescota at La Jolla Shores Beach; head up Frescota.

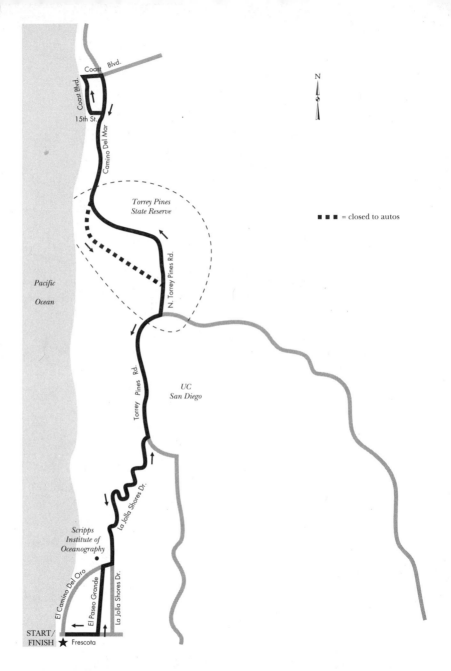

N

■ ■ ■ = closed to autos

Coast Blvd.

Coast Blvd.

15th St.

Camino Del Mar

Torrey Pines
State Reserve

N. Torrey Pines Rd.

Pacific

Ocean

Torrey Pines Rd.

UC
San Diego

La Jolla Shores Dr.

Scripps
Institute of
Oceanography

El Camino Del Oro

El Paseo Grande

La Jolla Shores Dr.

START/
FINISH   ★ Frescota

- 0.1 Straight onto El Paseo Grande.
- 0.5 Scripps Institute of Oceanography. Begin climb.
- 0.6 Left on La Jolla Shores Dr.
- 1.5 Summit.
- 1.9 UC San Diego. Left onto Torrey Pines Rd.
- 4.8 Torrey Pines Rd. becomes Camino Del Mar.
- 8.1 Del Mar. Left onto 15th St.
- 8.2 Left onto Coast Blvd.; train station, beach.
- 8.8 Right onto Camino Del Mar.
- 12.6 Right into Torrey Pines State Reserve; begin climb.
- 13.5 Summit.
- 13.7 Veer off bike path and onto N. Torrey Pines Rd.
- 14.7 Veer right, following Torrey Pines.
- 15.8 Right onto La Jolla Shores Dr.
- 17.1 Right onto El Paseo Grande.
- 17.6 Ride ends at La Jolla Shores Beach, where Frescota meets Camino Del Oro.

Central Coast

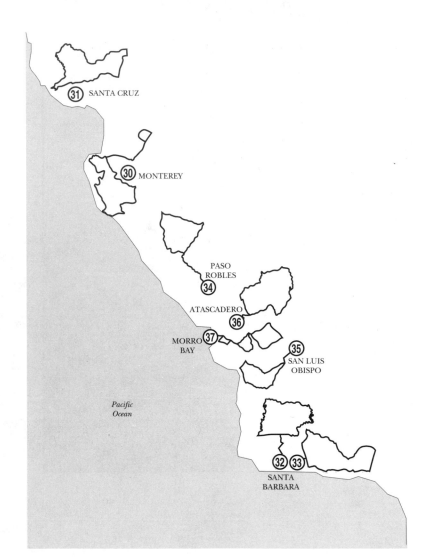

SANTA CRUZ ③

MONTEREY ③

PASO
ROBLES
③

ATASCADERO
③

MORRO ③
BAY

SAN LUIS
OBISPO ③

Pacific
Ocean

③ ③

SANTA
BARBARA

Central Coast

30. Pebble Beach Cruise 164
31. Boulder Creek Challenge 169
32. Painted Cave Challenge 174
33. Tour of Santa Barbara Ramble 179
34. Lake Nacimiento Classic 184
35. San Luis Valley Cruise 188
36. Oak Ridge Challenge 192
37. Morro Bay Ramble 197

30

Pebble Beach Cruise

Monterey—17 Mile Drive—Pebble Beach—
Pacific Grove—Monterey

There is a beautiful view from the Carmel grade, the curving
bay with the waves creaming on the sand, the dune country
around Seaside and right at the bottom of the hill, the warm
intimacy of the town.

—John Steinbeck, *Cannery Row*

The natural attributes of Monterey and its surrounding areas have become more developed since the days of Steinbeck, but its stunning beauty has somehow survived. Monterey is a salty canvas of windswept pines and crashing waves and gentle grades leading to limitless seascape vistas. As you pedal away from the crowds of the downtown area, the dramatic coastal landscape is enough to trigger that rare, euphoric feeling of being in the best of all possible places in the best of all possible ways—on your bike.

With the vast scope of things to see and do, the 28-mile Pebble Beach Cruise is the kind of ride that could take all day. And maybe it should. Leave your Greg LeMond attitude behind, and instead heft along your trusty camera. This is one ride you won't want to remember as a blur.

Your ride starts right outside Monterey at the Sand Dunes Beach parking lot. All you'll find here is a parking lot, a beach, and a bike path, but then, that's all you need, right? Besides, within 3 miles of the ride's start, you'll reach downtown Monterey, Fisherman's Wharf, Cannery Row, and every amenity—including "I Love Monterey" baseball caps and cotton candy—that you ever dreamed possible. The bustling, working-class wharf of the Cannery Row that John Steinbeck made famous now exists only in the text of his classic tale. Authenticity has made way for capitalism, resulting in a 1990s tourism amalgam of McDonald's eateries, trained monkeys, and street mimes.

If you can endure—maybe even get a kick out of—2 miles of true tackiness, the crowded bike path will begin to thin out and lead you to Ocean View Drive, one of the most sensational stretches of beach on the entire California coastline. As you cruise up the coast, make sure to unglue your eyes from the ocean long enough to check out the other side of the road, where virtually tame deer frolic on the famed Pebble Beach Golf Course.

After almost 4 miles of ocean, the road curves gently inland and brings you to the start of the 17 Mile Drive, which is chock-full of amazing vista points and gently rolling roads shaded by arching trees. Because this "drive" is one of the biggest tourist attractions in the entire area, you'll have to succumb to bureaucratic rigmarole by checking in with a ranger and signing a waiver stating that you'll be a good bicyclist and follow the rules and stay on designated roads. Although this stretch of tarmac is definitely not the stuff of secluded backroads, the overpowering grandeur of the surrounding land and sea makes it well worth the relatively minor hassle of sharing the road with car-driving tourists. And once you've experienced the two-wheeled version of this drive, with the salty wind whipping in your face and the rollercoaster hills pulling you effortlessly forward, you'll feel truly sorry for all those tourists cooped up in their mechanized boxes. By trading your Big Gulp and car stereo for a windbreaker and a Power Bar, you get to experience the 17 Mile Drive in a way that no car driver ever will.

The only major climb of the day comes as the road forks with an option of heading up to Highway 1 or dropping down into the overpriced, overcommercialized "hamlet" of Carmel. Your ride heads upward, past a cautionary sign that basically warns bicyclists that the hill ahead is going to kick their butts. The climb *is* steep, but if you've done this ride right, you've made lots of stops along the way to groove on the scenery, and you should be thoroughly rested for this 1.5-mile challenge. After you crest the hill and get onto Highway 1, you'll be on your way back to Monterey. Retrace your tread past glorious Ocean View Drive, congested Fisherman's Wharf, and, finally, back to the soft, squishy sound of waves against sand at Sand Dunes Beach.

The Basics

Start: Sand Dunes Beach parking lot. Exit Hwy. 1 at the Canyon Del Ray exit. Proceed under the freeway overpass to Sand Dunes Beach, across from the Monterey Beach Hotel. No restrooms in parking lot.

Length: 28 miles.

Terrain: Long, flat stretches and gently rolling hills. One major climb toward the end of the ride. Ultrascenic drives with fair amounts of traffic on weekends.

Food: No food mart at the ride's start, but food options galore in downtown Monterey. Restaurants at the Pebble Beach Resort if you're feeling fancy. Great après-ride Mexican food at Peppers on Forest Dr. in Monterey.

For more information: Velo Club Monterey, contact Joe Zoellin; (408) 899–0472.

Miles & Directions

- 0.0 From parking lot, ride under freeway overpass onto Cyn Del Ray.
- 0.1 Turn right onto bike path parallel to Del Monte.
- 0.9 Cross Roberts Ave.; begin Monterey Peninsula Recreation Trail.
- 2.6 Stay on bike path through Fisherman's Wharf; highly congested area.
- 4.7 End bike path; turn right onto Ocean View Dr. past Lovers' Point Park.
- 8.3 Right onto 17 Mile Dr.
- 8.5 Pebble Beach Ranger Station; bicyclists *must* sign in.

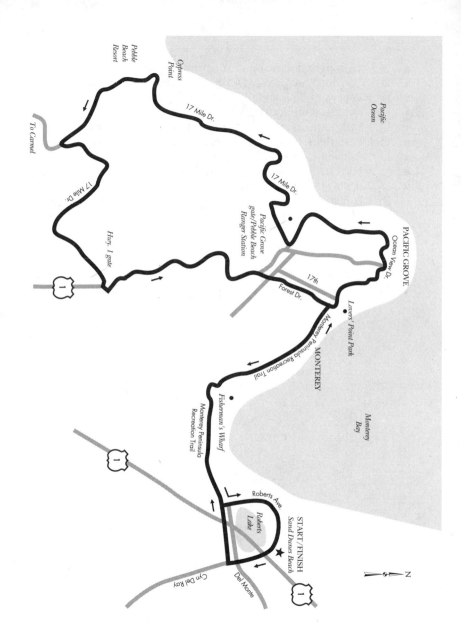

Pebble Beach Resort

Cypress Point

17 Mile Dr.

To Carmel

17 Mile Dr.

Hwy. 1 gate

17 Mile Dr.

Pacific Grove gate/Pebble Beach Ranger Station

Forest Dr.

17th

Pacific Ocean

PACIFIC GROVE

Ocean View Dr.

Lovers' Point Park

MONTEREY

Monterey Peninsula Recreation Trail

Fisherman's Wharf

Monterey Bay

Monterey Peninsula Recreation Trail

Roberts Ave.

Roberts Lake

Cyn Del Ray

Del Monte

START/FINISH
Sand Dunes Beach

N

- 9.5 Turn right, following 17 MILE DRIVE signs.
- 11.5 Continue on 17 Mile Dr.; don't follow BIKE ROUTE signs.
- 12.5 Veer right, following 17 MILE DRIVE signs.
- 13.1 Cypress Point lookout.
- 14.2 Path to the famous and oft-photographed Lone Cypress.
- 15.4 Turn right, following 17 Mile Dr. route.
- 15.8 Pebble Beach Resort.
- 15.9 Turn right, following 17 Mile Dr. route.
- 17.5 Begin steep ascent up to Hwy. 1.
- 18.9 Left at Hwy. 1 gate, then another immediate left onto Hwy. 68 toward Pacific Grove.
- 23.2 Left onto Forest Dr. to Lovers' Point Park. Cross Ocean View Dr. Right onto bike path.
- 27.4 Left at Comfort Inn onto Roberts Ave.
- 27.7 Left onto Canyon Del Ray.
- 28.0 End at Sand Dunes Beach parking lot.

31

Boulder Creek Challenge

Santa Cruz—Boulder Creek—Zayante—Felton—
Henry Cowell State Park—Santa Cruz

With my bike, I have the courage and resolve to go to places
I've never been. And then, without noticing, the bicycle trip
becomes a point of departure for other things. It's all part of
the lure and magic of the road.
                    —Elaine Mariolle, *California Bicyclist*

Serendipity. It's that unexpected bonus life throws at us every now
and then. Like finding $10 in the pocket of a jersey you haven't
worn in months. Or meeting your future spouse on a century ride.

It's not surprising that bike fanatics experience these serendipitous moments more often than the rest of the world. Every time
you mount your metal stallion, you're pedaling off on a new adventure, and the things that greet you around the bend or over a
summit are often unexpected, sometimes amazing, and—every
once in a while—life-changing.

Riding into the tiny mountain town of Boulder Creek is an experience of serendipitous proportions. From the cozy community
of Santa Cruz, you can look toward the tree-enshrouded mountains
and easily envision yourself pedaling up secluded roads through
corridors of redwoods. As you look hillward and think about your
ride, beautiful terrain seems almost a given. But on these quiet,
forested roads, what you probably *don't* expect to find is the sandal-
wearin', tofu-munchin' town of Boulder Creek, which appears out
of nowhere like some time-warped, psychedelic mirage. The town
is a modern-day refuge for real-life hippies—old and young alike—

who loll cross-legged on the sidewalks, surrounded by mountains and sheltered from the harshness of today's world. You almost expect to see a tie-dyed cloud hovering in the air above.

Although the city of Santa Cruz retains some of its hippie roots, the true believers have fled to the mountains of Boulder Creek. And on your bike from downtown, it'll be a hilly 24 miles to visit them up there. The climbing begins almost immediately as you head toward UC Santa Cruz and are immediately engulfed by a sea of redwoods. It's a gradual uphill grind that lasts for 15 miles but is made a bit easier by the generally gentle grade of the road and the ever-changing landscape—which keeps your mind off the dull pain of throbbing legs. From the top, distant mountains provide the perfect backdrop for the kind of picturesque ridge riding that makes you wonder whether you should laugh, cry, or hop off your bike and drop to the ground for a moment of reverence.

If you're not into the peace, love, and organic food scene in Boulder Creek, there's yet another good reason to stop here: The climbing isn't over yet for this ride, and this will be your last chance to get water and food for at least 23 miles. From Boulder Creek, 5 scenic and secluded miles lie between you and your next climb. By the time Bear Creek Road begins to arch and pull its way up the mountain, you're enveloped in a forest as thick and wild and brown and moist as something you'd find in the Amazon. You are not, however, anywhere near the Amazon, and the small and unassuming wineries that are tucked into the folds of the forest serve as a locale reminder. The unique climate and terrain of Northern California make it one of the few places in the world that redwood trees can call home and in which vineyards can prosper.

When you pass the Byington Winery at mile 32.1, you're almost home free. From here it's less than 1 mile before the road coils into a spiraling descent. It's not exactly mindless cruising, however. The road, which snakes narrowly down the mountain, with little room for more than one car, requires some concentration and a lot of good technique in order to get the most enjoyment out of it (and to prevent crashing).

There's nothing but nature for 14 plummeting, plunging miles as you work your way out of the mountains and back toward town.

From Felton, city life begins to thicken all around you. After you've passed the north boundary of Henry Cowell State Park, it'll be you and the cars dropping back into Santa Cruz. But this isn't necessarily a bad thing. As you descend, smell the *lattes*. Envision a deli sandwich and a sidewalk cafe. Click your heels three times and say "There's no place like home." You're almost there.

The Basics

Start: Spokesman Bicycles at Cathcart St. and Cedar St. in downtown Santa Cruz.
Length: 53.4 miles.
Terrain: Major climbs, steep descents, virtually no flat sections. Secluded roads, often one-lane. Heavy traffic for 3 miles on Hwy. 236.
Food: There are plenty of food options in Santa Cruz, of course. A market and a restaurant are in Boulder Creek at mile 24.2. After that, no food or water is available until Felton, at mile 47.2. (In desperation, you may be able to find a hose in someone's yard.)
For more information: Santa Cruz Visitors Information Center, 701 Front St., Santa Cruz, CA 95061; (408) 425–1234.

Miles & Directions

- 0.0 From the Spokesman Bicycles on Cathcart St. at Cedar St. in downtown Santa Cruz, take a right onto Cedar.
- 0.4 Right onto Center St.; then an immediate left onto Mission St.
- 0.7 Right onto King St.
- 0.8 Right onto Storey St.
- 1.0 Left onto High St. to UC Santa Cruz; begin climbing.
- 2.0 Pass UC Santa Cruz on your right.
- 3.3 Road narrows, High St. becomes Empire Grade.
- 11.8 Pass Bonny Doon Village Airport.
- 17.0 Descent begins.
- 18.4 Right onto Jamison Creek Rd.; major descent!

China Grade

Jamison Creek Rd.

236

9

BOULDER CREEK

Bear Creek Rd.

Bear Creek Rd.

Bear Creek Rd.

Summit Rd.

Upper Zayante Rd.

Empire Grade

Bonny Doon Village Airport

E. Zayante Rd.

Mt. Herman Rd.

FELTON

Graham Hill Rd.

N

Empire Grade

UC Santa Cruz

Ocean St.

Storey St.

Mission St.

Cedar St.

Soquel Ave.

King St.

Mission St.

Cathcart St.

START/FINISH
Spokesman Bicycles

SANTA
CRUZ

- 21.5 Right on Hwy. 236 (unmarked). Heavy traffic; no shoulder.
- 24.2 Boulder Creek. Left onto Hwy. 9.
- 24.5 Right onto Bear Creek Rd.
- 29.4 Begin climb.
- 32.1 Pass Byington Winery.
- 33.7 Descent begins. **Careful:** Very twisty!
- 34.7 Right onto Summit Rd.; one-lane road.
- 34.9 Right onto Upper Zayante Rd.
- 38.8 Continue straight through intersection.
- 43.5 Stop sign; continue straight.
- 45.4 Intersection with W. Zayante; continue straight.
- 47.2 Felton. Right onto Mt. Herman Rd. Left onto Graham Hill Rd.
- 48.1 Pass north boundary of Henry Cowell State Park.
- 51.6 Veer right onto Ocean St.
- 52.0 Cross under Hwy. 101; veer right, following Ocean St.
- 52.8 Right onto Soquel Ave.
- 53.2 Right onto Pacific.
- 53.3 Left onto Cathcart.
- 53.4 Ride ends at Spokesman Bicycles on Cathcart at Cedar.

32

Painted Cave Challenge

*Mission Santa Barbara—Rattlesnake Canyon Park—
La Cumbre Peak—Chumash Painted Cave State
Park—Knapp's Castle—Mission Santa Barbara*

> *If ye would go up high, then use your own legs! Do not get
> yourselves carried aloft.*
> —Friedrich Wilhelm Nietzsche

If Gibraltar Road had a face, it would be smirking. This cocky ribbon of tarmac is unrelenting in its ascent through the Santa Ynez
Mountains above Santa Barbara. It's the kind of road that chips
away at any hopes of ever reaching a summit. You can almost hear
the pavement laughing diabolically as you round each bend—as
you search in vain for that telltale blue horizon—only to find yet
another uphill grade.

Depending upon the kind of rider you are, the prospect of this
ride's demanding demeanor will either send you into orbit or an-
chor you even more firmly to the flatlands. But whatever your feelings about grueling uphill grinds, this is a climb that is worth
toughing out. The rewards from the top are unparalleled, and your
viewing ecstasy is all the greater when you've got the added bonus
of natural endorphins coursing through your veins.

The ride begins at Velo Pro bike shop in the downtown Santa
Barbara shopping district of State Street, where cafes and bookstores line the busy road. After you've ridden for 2 miles, the beginning of your ascent is marked by the curvy, sensuous architecture
of Mission Santa Barbara. Built in 1786 with the help of Chumash

Native Americans, the mission is perched upon the first tiny foothills of your impending mountain climb.

For the next 11 miles, all of your pedaling will be uphill. At first a residential jaunt with fairly mellow grades, your route passes a sampling of the beautiful, prestigious homes tucked away in the Montecito hills. Once you pass the Sheffield Reservoir and turn onto Mountain Drive, however, you leave these residences behind for the solitude—as well as the challenge—of Gibraltar Road. Although a monastic retreat center and a few dirt driveways dropping off the side of the mountain offer brief reminders of civilization, you'll basically be alone with your thoughts and your legs and your pain as you twist higher and higher up the mountain.

At mile 10.9 Gibraltar intersects with Camino Cielo. The road isn't marked, but you'll know you're there when you see the big brown sign listing distances to various locations. In the middle of nowhere, it's signs like these that offer the reassurance necessary to keep pushing forward. They remind you that you *are* going somewhere, and that your journey is finite; it is numerically marked. Armed with this knowledge, you can feel more certain that the miles will pass and you will reach your destination. You *will* get there.

From Camino Cielo you'll have another 1 mile or so of climbing before you top out at 3,985-foot La Cumbre Peak. On a sunny day from this mountaintop (and there are lots of sunny days), you are surrounded by a clear expansiveness, an outreaching sky. Snuggled far below this wall of mountains, the Santa Ynez Valley stretches before your eyes. Turn the other way and you'll see Santa Barbara reaching lazily toward the shores of the Pacific.

Back on your bike, you'll find the backside of this ride to be even steeper than the ascent. Dramatically sharp switchbacks drop downward with conviction. All you have to do is career back to earth at a deliberate, steady pace—with your fingers consistently massaging your brakes. When you turn off Camino Cielo at Painted Cave Road, you'll see the windmills that spin above Jane Fonda's ranch, and you'll have a chance to take a side trip to Knapp's Castle. There's a narrow trail from the road (public property) that leads to the castle ruins, and it's just a 0.25-mile hike.

Drop from here through thick groves of arching chaparrals, and you'll soon be closing in on one of this ride's major sightseeing highlights, the Chumash Painted Cave State Park. (Funny how all your great excuses to stop riding are on the descent, huh?) This minuscule state park was erected solely to preserve the vivid cave paintings done centuries ago by Santa Barbara's Chumash Native Americans.

When Painted Cave Road becomes San Marcos Road, the rush of automobiles and the unnatural pastels of looming hilltop homes mark your entrance back to civilization. Upon reaching Cathedral Oaks Boulevard, be prepared for rolling hills and houses with oh-so-tempting orange trees that lean lusciously toward the road, flaunting their juicy bounty before your hunger-crazed eyes. If you can resist plucking fruit from someone's private stash, you'll probably be better off. You're in a respectable neighborhood now, and most likely you're looking less than respectable by this point. Best of all, you're less than 10 miles away from downtown Santa Barbara, where you can feast on just about anything your heart desires. Did you remember to bring your snack money? If not, what the hell. Get on your bike and get back to those orange trees.

The Basics

Start: Velo Pro bike shop at State St. and Ortega St. in downtown Santa Barbara.

Length: 35.2 miles.

Terrain: Steep hills almost the entire way. In the mountains: narrow roads with tight switchbacks and very little traffic. Moderate traffic on Hwy. 192.

Food: No food or water along the way. Stock up before the ride. There are plenty of postride restaurants and cafes on State St.

For more information: Goleta Valley Cycling Club; (805) 684–6060.

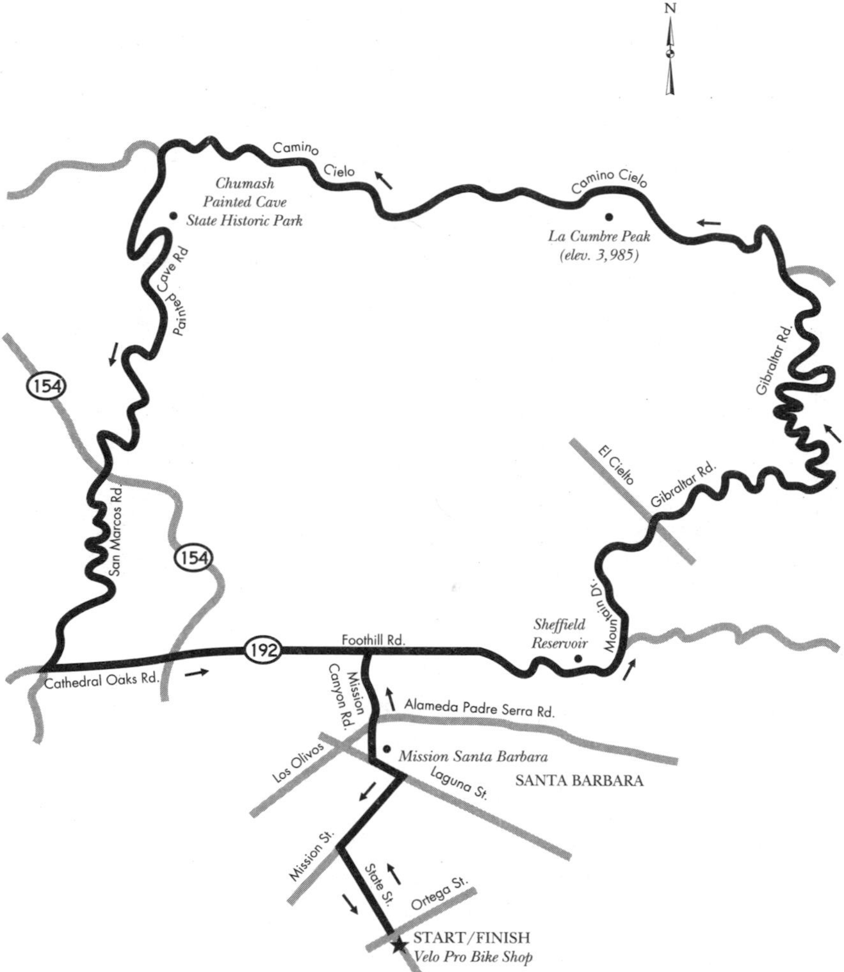

N

Camino Cielo

Chumash
Painted Cave
State Historic Park

Camino Cielo

La Cumbre Peak
(elev. 3,985)

Painted Cave Rd.

154

Gibraltar Rd.

San Marcos Rd.

154

El Cielo

Gibraltar Rd.

Foothill Rd.

Sheffield
Reservoir

Mountain Dr.

192

Cathedral Oaks Rd.

Mission Canyon Rd.

Alameda Padre Serra Rd.

Los Olivos

Mission Santa Barbara

Laguna St.

SANTA BARBARA

Mission St.

State St.

Ortega St.

★ START/FINISH
Velo Pro Bike Shop

Miles & Directions

- 0.0 Velo Pro bike shop at Ortega St. and State St. East on State St.
- 1.3 Right onto Mission St.
- 1.7 Left onto Laguna St.
- 2.0 Mission Santa Barbara. Follow Los Olivos to Mission Canyon Rd.; climbing begins.
- 2.6 Right onto Foothill (Hwy. 192).
- 3.5 Left onto Mountain Dr.
- 3.9 Left onto Mountain Dr. at filtration plant (Sheffield Reservoir).
- 4.1 Right onto Gibraltar.
- 4.5 Intersection with El Cielto. Continue on Gibraltar; climbing gets steeper.
- 10.9 Left onto Camino Cielo.
- 12.0 Summit at La Cumbre Peak.
- 20.3 Left on Painted Cave Rd.; all-out descending begins.
- 23.6 Cross Hwy. 154; Painted Cave Rd. becomes San Marcos Rd.
- 27.4 Left onto Cathedral Oaks Rd.; traffic thickens.
- 29.6 Cross under Hwy. 154; Cathedral Oaks Blvd. becomes Foothill Rd.
- 33.3 Mission Santa Barbara. Mission Canyon Rd. becomes Los Olivos.
- 33.5 Left onto Laguna St.
- 33.9 Right onto Mission St.
- 35.2 Ride ends at Velo Pro bike shop.

33

Tour of Santa Barbara Ramble

Downtown—Stearn's Wharf—Pacific Ocean—
Montecito—Mission Santa Barbara—Downtown

> *My life is like a stroll upon the beach,/As near the ocean's*
> *edge as I can go.*
>   —Henry David Thoreau, *The Fisher's Boy*

Twilight in the Montecito hills is like hovering above a glimmering birthday cake. High atop the glistening town of Santa Barbara, you are at once giant and powerful, yet also humbled and awed by the magical beauty of a twinkling vista. In the amber hues of dusk, the hills of Montecito catch gentle breezes rolling off the Pacific. The tropical warmth of the city below is replaced by a soft, benevolent chill that urges you to keep moving, to keep spinning downward to your deliciously brilliant destination—a vibrant city just waiting to be gobbled up like a sweet and rewarding dessert.

But if Santa Barbara is a birthday cake, it's not one of those heavy, gooey, ready-made numbers from the grocery store—it's more like a light and expensive torte. Its downtown is immaculate and sophisticated, all done up in red adobe, white stucco, and Mediterranean charm. And while Santa Barbara is somewhat of an elite Southern California playground, it is also home to bike-riding students from UC Santa Barbara, Birkenstock-wearin' hippies, and lots of wanderers and random homeless people. So whether you ride a $4,000 titanium wonder or a fifty-pound beach cruiser, you and your bike will probably blend right in.

Your ride begins and ends at the quintessential before-and-after bike ride locale: a hip, hangin'-out cafe with gourmet coffee and all-natural food. The tour is an 11.7-mile sightseeing extravaganza, but it's something that can be enjoyed by visitors and locals alike. As a tourist, you could spend all day covering these miles; there's so much to see and do that stopping along the way is irresistible. If, however, you're just in it for the ride, you can probably cover the distance in under an hour. Try it as a twilight ride after work: It's a great way to unwind after a long and busy day, and there's something absolutely magical about a Santa Barbara sunset, no matter how many times you've seen it before. (**Important safety tip:** Make sure to bring a light if you ride in the evening.)

Less than 0.5 mile after you clip into your pedals on State Street, the congested road opens up to a limitless expanse of ocean. The Pacific is at its best here, tumultuous and vital—with everyone from seafarers to volleyball players sharing its coast—but still as clean and sparkling as Santa Barbara itself. Beyond the shoreline anchored sailboats dot the surf, holding fast to their positions as they rise and fall with the swell of the waves. And on the horizon huge freighters can be spotted inching their way across what seems to be the edge of the world.

Immediately in front of you, at the intersection of Cabarillo and State streets, you'll see Stearn's Wharf, the oldest wharf still in use on the entire West Coast. From here you can pick up the bike path (which looks like nothing more than a sidewalk at first) for 1 mile of shoreline cycling. The bike path commands relatively slow riding as you weave your way through walkers, joggers, and skaters. But grooving along seems appropriate here, as you'll most likely want to check out the interesting people and take in the mind-blowing beauty. Weekends are especially lively at the beach. Arts and crafts stretch as far as the eye can see, and if you're lucky, you'll get to witness the band of wild-eyed hippies who converge on the grass and flail about maniacally to the beat of their bongos.

Things get more high-toned as you make your way to the up-scale community of Montecito, where wine bars and restaurants with chichi names like *Le Expensive Château* line the perfectly land-scaped Coast Village Road. Chances are, you won't be able to dine in Montecito in your sweaty Lycra, but there is a grocery store right on Coast Village, the main road.

As you continue inland, the route becomes more wooded and residential. Long driveways lead to hidden homes, and it's here that the climbing begins. A hearty 2-mile heave into the Montecito hills gets under way with the start of Alameda Padre Serra Road. As your breathing quickens and your legs perk up to the challenge, you'll be rising higher and higher above the oceanside city that you came from. Keep in mind that this is not a head-down-and-hammer type of climb. In fact, if you take it slow, it's actually a rather gentle ascent. Besides, if you get too engrossed in climbing, you'll miss your chance to devour the delectable views set out in front of you.

Less than 1 mile after you summit the climb, you'll pedal upon Mission Santa Barbara. With its pristine, adobe-style architecture and voluptuous beauty, the structure alone is enough to provoke a religious experience. The mission was built in 1786 with the help of Chumash Native Americans, and its architectural style has been adopted as the classic Santa Barbara look. If you can find somewhere to lock your bike, you can take a guided tour for only $2.00.

The mission is just a few short blocks from State Street, which serves as the hub of Santa Barbara's recently renovated downtown. For a bustling shopping district, this area is incredibly tasteful—and it wins even more points for its well-defined bike lane and myriad bike racks. There's a good bike shop, Velo Pro, at the corner of State and Ortega streets, and from there it's a quick spin down to the Coffee Roasting Company where you started. Back at the airy, expansive cafe, you can sip your coffee under cathedral ceilings and soak up the pristine Santa Barbara ambience, keeping in mind that it's all the more pristine when you tour it on two wheels.

The Basics

Start: Coffee Roasting Company, 321 Motor Way, at State St. and Guiterrez St. in downtown Santa Barbara.

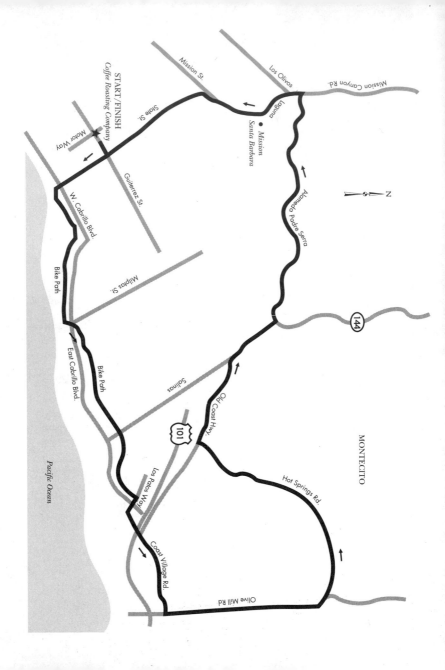

Length: 11.7 miles.
Terrain: Mostly flat, with one 2-mile climb; moderately heavy traffic, but there's a bike path or bike lane for 75 percent of the route.
Food: You can get all the food you want in downtown Santa Barbara. There's also a grocery store in Montecito at mile 2.8. From there you'll find no more food or water stops until you reach the mission, at mile 9.3.
For more information: Visitor Center, 1 Santa Barbara St., Santa Barbara, CA 93101; (805) 965–3021.

Miles & Directions

- 0.0 From the Coffee Roasting Company at State St. and Guiterrez St., turn right onto State St. toward the ocean.
- 0.3 Left onto W. Cabrillo Blvd.; veer onto sidewalk, which becomes bike path.
- 1.4 Cross Cabrillo Blvd. at Milpitas; stay on bike path.
- 2.5 Veer right off bike path onto E. Cabrillo Blvd. at Los Patos Way.
- 2.7 Veer right under Hwy. 101 to Coast Village Rd.
- 2.8 Montecito.
- 3.6 Coast Village Rd. ends at Hwy. 101 and Olive Mill Rd; turn left onto Olive Mill Rd. (don't follow Pacific Coast Bike Rte. onto Hwy. 101!).
- 4.2 Left onto Hot Springs Rd.
- 5.0 Right onto Old Coast Hwy.
- 6.0 Right onto Salinas.
- 6.7 Straight at traffic circle. Salinas becomes Alameda Padre Serra; begin climb.
- 8.7 Summit.
- 9.2 Straight onto Los Olivos at stop sign.
- 9.3 Mission Santa Barbara.
- 9.4 Left onto Laguna.
- 9.5 Right onto Mission.
- 10.0 Left onto State St.
- 11.7 Right onto Guiterrez; immediate left onto Motor Way. Ride ends at the Coffee Roasting Company.

34

Lake Nacimiento Classic

Paso Robles—Nacimiento Lake—
San Antonio Reservoir—Lockwood—Paso Robles

Whenever I'm alone, I tend to brood,/but when I'm out on
my bike, it's a different mood./I leave my brain at home, get
up on the saddle./No hangin' around, I don't diddle-daddle.
—Luka Bloom, "The Acoustic Motorbike"

There's a Denny's restaurant right off Highway 101 in the smallish town of Paso Robles. And there's a nice guy who's working there and saying his life isn't going anywhere 'cause he's stuck in this ho-dunk town.

If only that guy had a bike.

Paso Robles may not exactly be a kickin' destination loaded with entertainment value, but the landscape is fertile and inviting and cleansing. Wide-open roads lined with almond and walnut trees curve through the hills to Nacimiento Lake. Vineyards and farmlands spread from quiet country roads and give you the space and freedom to think, to regroup and rediscover the possibilites of life and the world. Corny? Perhaps. But ask the myriad bicyclists who take to these roads why they ride here. You're likely to get a similar answer.

The Lake Nacimiento Classic dives into the unexplored farmland of the Central Coast, an area with so many backroads and so few cars that you'll feel like you've gone to road bikers' heaven. Keep in mind, however, that the Central Coast is extremely hot in the summer, and shade is a precious commodity on many of these roads, making spring and fall the best times to plan a ride.

The rolling road out to Nacimiento Lake is filled with cyclists and marks the first part of your journey. To make this ride a cruise instead of a classic, you could head out to the lake, do some recreating, and then simply turn around and head back to Paso Robles. If you continue on from the Nacimiento Lake Resort, North Shore, you'll be faced with a steep climb that eventually drops you down into a virtually deserted stretch of vast, flat open land. You probably won't run into too many bicyclists out here. It's the kind of place where you're more likely to encounter a tractor than a car.

As you move near the Lockwood city limits at mile 40.3, you move away from the barren plains and back into the fertile, tree-covered hills surrounding Nacimiento Lake. While making the transition back to greenness, gnarled, barren trees stand stoically next to more prosperous ones, posing a question mark—as if to cast some uncertainty on the promise of fertility rendered by the ever-deepening vibrancy of the terrain. Just as you think you've successfully flown from the barren fields, you pass another twisted dead tree.

But as you climb amid the oaks and continue upward through the woods, an unmistakable verdancy returns. You can almost taste and feel the richness of the soil, the bounty of the lake. After nearly 12 miles of tough climbs, you are treated to incredible views from high above the San Antonio Reservoir, which sparkles below and marks your return back to Paso Robles.

From the reservoir you'll be connected once again to the undulations of Lake Nacimiento Road, and you can glide back to town tired from the long miles and tough climbs but refueled both mentally and physically.

The Basics

Start: Paso Robles (off Hwy. 101) at 24th St. and Spring St.
Length: 80 miles.
Terrain: Hilly; steep climbs; some extended flat areas. Open roads; little traffic most of the way. Very little shade.
Food: Stock up in Paso Robles; otherwise, you're limited to the

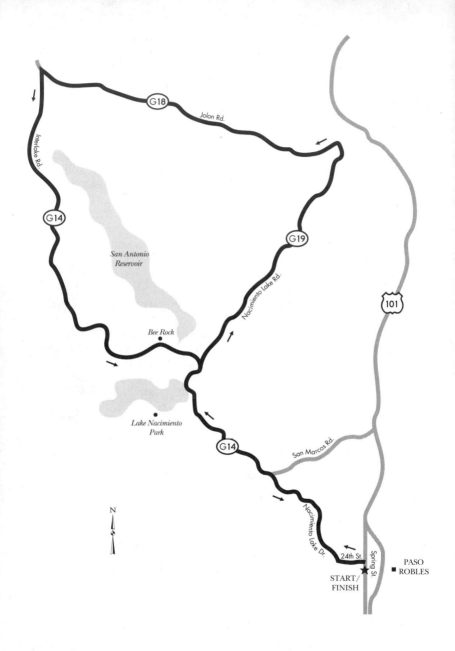

Western Oak Restaurant at mile 29.3, a store in Lockwood at mile 40.3, or the Bee Rock store at mile 57.9.

For more information: San Luis Obispo Bike Club; (805) 543–5973.

Miles & Directions

- 0.0 From 24th St. and Spring St., go west on 24th St.
- 0.4 Veer right, following Nacimiento Lake Dr.
- 6.1 Straight past San Marcos Rd.
- 8.1 Right onto Nacimiento Lake Rd. (unmarked).
- 8.2 Begin climb.
- 9.2 Summit.
- 15.8 Right, following G-14 to Lake Nacimiento/San Antonio Reservoir Recreation Area.
- 16.2 Lake Nacimiento Resort, North Shore. Begin steep climb.
- 17.2 Summit.
- 17.5 Straight past Interlake Rd.
- 19.3 Veer right, following Nacimiento Lake Rd.
- 26.4 Left onto Jolon Rd.
- 35.5 Straight past New Pleyto Rd.
- 40.3 Lockwood city limits.
- 41.7 Left onto G-14.
- 48.2 Begin climb.
- 49.2 Summit.
- 54.7 Begin climb.
- 55.7 Summit.
- 59.2 Begin climb.
- 60.8 Summit.
- 61.2 Lake Nacimiento/San Antonio Reservoir.
- 62.5 Right onto Nacimiento Lake Rd.
- 71.9 Right onto Nacimiento Lake Dr.
- 79.6 Nacimiento Lake Dr. becomes 24th St.
- 80.0 Ride ends at 24th St. and Spring St.

35

San Luis Valley Cruise

San Luis Obispo—Arroyo Grande—Grover Beach—
Pismo Beach—Edna—San Luis Obispo

I owe my soul to each fork in the road, each misleading sign,
'cause even in solitude, no bitter attitude can dissolve my
sweetest find.

—Poi Dog Pondering, "Thanksgiving"

From a young hipster on a Harley-Davidson to a sun-dried farmer on a John Deere. From a flurry of cafes, bookstores, and restaurants to the wide expanse of an open field. In San Luis Obispo, city and country rub close familial elbows. It's the kind of place where you can ride from the busy, rambunctious streets to serene roads in less than ten minutes. And don't think cyclists haven't figured this out. As soon as you roll out of town, you'll find yourself sharing the road with more cyclists than cars.

Your ride starts on the heavily trafficked streets of downtown San Luis Obispo before heading out to the more countrified Orcutt Road, which weaves through the golden hills of the Central Coast. At Lopez Drive you'll turn left and head toward Arroyo Grande under the shade of lush oak trees, which soon give way to the area's more typical amber hills. When you finally emerge from the countryside and find yourself in the seaside town of Arroyo Grande, it's just a 4-mile ride to Highway 1, where the Pacific Ocean spreads out before you and expands the possibilities of the world in a way those inland hills never could.

But after a short jog along the beach, your route heads back inland as Price Canyon Road slices through the vast, open countryside. And when you hit Highway 277, you're home free—it's an easy 6 miles back to San Luis Obispo. There you can patronize one of the myriad hip cafes and ponder the virtues of both city and country, of both rolling, fertile farmland and endless ocean. Because in San Luis Obispo, you don't have to choose; you can have it all.

The Basics

Start: Downtown San Luis Obispo, accessible via Hwy. 101.
Length: 32.6 miles.
Terrain: Rolling hills; mainly quiet roads, some busy sections.
Food: There's a health food store right on the route in Pismo Beach, along with whatever else your heart desires. There are also plenty of options at the ride start/finish in San Luis Obispo.
For more information: San Luis Obispo Bike Club; (805) 543–5973.

Miles & Directions

- 0.0 From Higuera St. and Broad St., go left (south) on Broad St.
- 1.5 Left onto Orcutt Rd.
- 2.3 Veer right at stop sign, following Orcutt Rd.
- 3.3 Left at stop sign, following Orcutt Rd.
- 10.9 Lopez Water Treatment Plant.
- 11.5 Right onto Lopez Dr. to Arroyo Grande.
- 14.2 Straight past Huasna to Arroyo Grande.
- 15.0 Arroyo Grande city limits. Lopez Dr. becomes Huasna Rd.
- 15.8 Left onto Stanley; road becomes E. Branch St.
- 16.1 Downtown Arroyo Grande.
- 16.8 Cross Hwy. 101; road becomes Grand Ave.
- 19.5 Right onto Hwy. 1.
- 21.0 Right onto Hinds Ave.

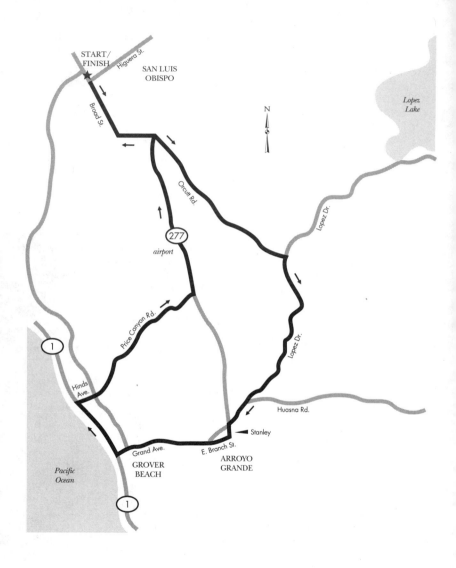

START/
FINISH

Higuera St.

SAN LUIS
OBISPO

Broad St.

Lopez
Lake

N

Orcutt Rd.

277

airport

Lopez Dr.

Price Canyon Rd.

Lopez Dr.

Hinds
Ave.

Huasna Rd.

Stanley

1

Grand Ave.

E. Branch St.

Pacific
Ocean

GROVER
BEACH

ARROYO
GRANDE

1

- 21.2 Cross Hwy. 101; road becomes Price Canyon Rd.
- 26.1 Left onto Hwy. 277 to San Luis Obispo.
- 29.5 San Luis Obispo airport.
- 30.7 San Luis Obispo city limits. Hwy. 277 intersects with Orcutt; becomes Broad St.
- 32.6 Ride ends at Broad St. and Higuera St.

36

Oak Ridge Challenge

*Atascadero—Morro Bay—Cayucos—Santa Rita
Ridge—Oak Ridge—Templeton—Atascadero*

> *Those green-robed senators of mighty woods,/Tall oaks,
> branch-charmed by the earnest stars,/Dream, and so dream
> all night without a stir.*
>
> —John Keats, *Hyperion*

Atascadero is a funny little city, punctuated by quaint farmhouses,
an old-style town square, and new-style strip malls. But get out of
town—which takes only about 3 miles of pedaling—and you
quickly catapult yourself into the throes of nature. Oak trees dripping with moss reach down to brush your face, quiet ranches nes-
tle among rolling hills, and at times you hear nothing save the
rush of the wind.

The Oak Ridge Challenge encompasses all this and more. The
delight begins at mile 6.2, when you're treated to the virtually carless Old Morro Road. This venerable cracked road wends through
the shaded sanctuary of a deeply wooded landscape. Rejoining
Morro Road (and cars) at mile 7.9, you'll have nearly 12 miles of ef-
fortless descending as you twist through the woods and down to
the beachfront town of Morro Bay.

As you drop into town, you can see above the often-foggy bay to
the limitless blue distance extending outward with the Pacific Ocean.
Down in Morro Bay you can't get this perspective, and the town
feels creepy—almost mystical—as the towering Morro Rock looms
hazily in the forefront, casting its stony presence over the town.

After a few miles along the coast, the route turns back inland again, and before long you're back to the solitude of a hilly forest of moss-draped oak. Only this time there's a bit more challenge. The pavement ends. You hit dirt. Loose gravel. This will be your traveling surface for the next 9.7 difficult, hilly miles. And while these miles can be ridden on a road bike, you may want to consider using a hybrid or mountain bike on this ride to better tackle the loose-gravel, uphill climbing.

As you ascend through the hills and thicker into the woods, all signs of civilization disappear. There are no cars. No homes. Expect to see only the deer and squirrels that inhabit the forest. Or perhaps a fairy underneath a mushroom cap: The deeper you ride in, the more you become a part of this world and all the magic that surrounds it. The summit of Santa Rita Road yields a powerful, windswept view of soft hills peeling off into the distance, as well as the narrow dirt road that will lead you back to civilization.

When you're reunited with asphalt, you'll have approximately 10 easy miles back to Atascadero, including one particularly fun stretch of rollers on Templeton Road. When you get back to Atascadero, you can slide off your bike and onto the inviting lawn of the town square, where the ride ends.

The Basics

Start: Atascadero town square, accessible via Hwy. 101.
Length: 50.4 miles.
Terrain: Hilly. Many extended climbs; rough roads, including 9 miles of loose gravel.
Food: There's a large grocery store on El Camino Real right before your turn onto Hwy. 41; there are also plenty of quaint restaurants in Morro Bay, including a good selection of seafood joints at Fisherman's Wharf; after Morro Bay, you're on your own.
For more information: San Luis Obispo Bike Club; (805) 543–5973.

Miles & Directions

- 0.0 W. Mall and Fountain Way. Go south on W. Mall to El Camino Real.
- 0.1 Left onto El Camino Real.
- 2.8 Right onto Hwy. 41W to Morro Bay.
- 6.2 Left onto Old Morro Rd.
- 6.4 Begin climb.
- 7.3 Summit.
- 7.9 Left onto Morro Rd. (Hwy 41W).
- 19.1 Morro Bay city limits.
- 19.5 Cross Main St.

Option: For a scenic tour of Morro Bay that'll add 19.7 miles to this tour, follow the directions for the Morro Bay Ramble, page 196, which starts and ends on Main St. and Hwy. 1.

- 19.6 Under Hwy. 1 to beaches.
- 20.8 Pacific Ocean; turnaround point.
- 22.0 Left onto Main St.
- 23.9 Get onto Hwy. 1 at Yerba Buena St.
- 24.3 Cuyana city limits.
- 25.1 Right onto Old Creek Rd.
- 25.3 Begin climb.
- 26.7 Summit at Whale Rock Reservoir.
- 30.0 Right onto Santa Rita Rd.
- 31.2 Pavement ends; loose gravel for 9.7 miles.
- 34.6 Begin climbing.
- 36.6 Summit.
- 40.4 Left onto Santa Rita Rd.
- 40.8 Right onto Vineyard Dr.
- 41.4 Cross Hwy. 101; road becomes Templeton Rd.
- 41.9 Right onto Templeton Rd.
- 47.6 Sharp right, following Hwy. 41 across Salinas River Bridge.
- 47.7 Atascadero city limits.
- 47.8 Right onto Sycamore Rd. (Hwy. 41).
- 48.9 Left, following Hwy. 41 (Capistrano Hwy.).
- 50.1 Capistrano Hwy. becomes W. Mall.
- 50.4 Ride ends at W. Mall and Fountain Way.

37

Morro Bay Ramble

Morro Bay—Los Osos—Morro Bay

You don't need a weatherman to know which way the wind blows.

—Bob Dylan, *Subterranean Homesick Blues*

Morro Bay stretches eerily along the fog-enshrouded shores of the Pacific Ocean. A string of inviting inns hug the rocky beachfront for just a few short miles, until the end of town is marked abruptly by a monstrously large rock peeking above the fog line and standing solidly in defiance as waves crash chaotically around it. Beyond the ocean one has only to venture a few miles inland before encountering the sun-drenched fields that are characteristic of much of the inland Central Coast.

The Morro Bay Ramble is a rollicking tour, from the eerie, uncertain atmosphere of the coast to the sunshiny promise of golden fields. The ride begins at the towering formation of Morro Rock, part of a string of volcanic peaks stretching along the Central Coast and dubbed the Seven Sisters.

A 2-mile roll through town brings you to Morro Bay State Park, located right on the edge of the sailboat-dotted bay. Tall pine trees and slippery, waxy eucalyptus shade your journey as languid waves lap up against the marshy shores of the bay. And it's not until you turn onto Los Osos Valley Road at mile 7 that the fog disappears and the air dries up with the warmth of the sun.

The 3-mile stretch on Los Osos Valley Road is laden with traffic but provides a good shoulder for cycling. At mile 10 a flower farm paints the earth with electric tones of orange, pink, purple, and gold and also marks your turn onto one of the most lovely back-roads in all of California: Turri Road. This quietly voluptuous road rolls gently upward through green-carpeted hills as it makes its way to Morro Bay. As you ascend through the curving hills, the formidable Morro Rock juts into the horizon and fog begins to roll violently over the hills, marking your return to Morro Bay.

Entering the Morro Bay State Park again, you'll take the steep but short climb up to Black Hill Golf Course before dropping quickly into town and down to Embarcadero Street, where seafood restaurants, crowds, and the trappings of tourism remind you that this isn't *The Ancient Mariner,* but more like the story of the 1990s, where commercialism takes precedence over naturalism. But this little reality jaunt is short-lived (less than 0.5 mile). And, of course, it's not so terribly bad. When you finish the ride in another 1.5 miles, you may find yourself heading back over there for some wharf-style seafood. And that just may be the perfect ending to your alternately sunny and salty ride.

The Basics

Start: Junction of Hwy. 1 and Hwy. 41 in Morro Bay.
Length: 19.7 miles.
Terrain: Rolling hills, some steep pitches, some flat sections. Mostly quiet roads; some heavily trafficked sections on Los Osos Valley Rd. and South Bay Blvd.
Food: Myriad restaurants in Morro Bay; some food options of lesser quality in Los Osos.
For more information: San Luis Obispo Bike Club; (805) 543–5973.

Miles & Directions

- 0.0 From Hwy. 41 and Main St., go south on Main St. toward downtown Morro Bay.
- 0.9 Downtown Morro Bay.

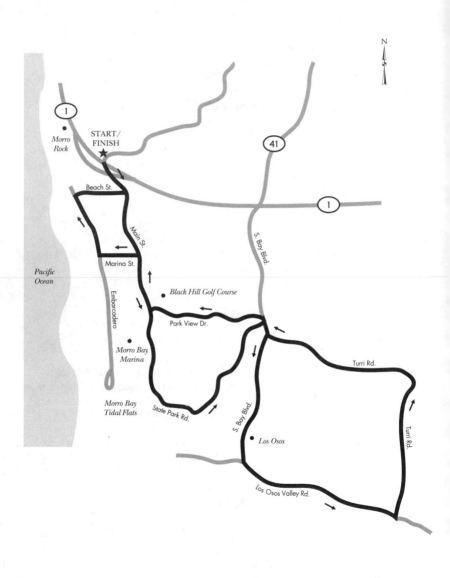

- 2.0 Enter Morro Bay State Park; proceed straight past road to golf course.
- 2.6 Morro Bay Marina and Bayside Cafe.
- 3.7 Right onto S. Bay Blvd. (unmarked).
- 5.5 Los Osos city limits.
- 7.0 Left onto Los Osos Valley Rd.
- 10.0 Left onto Turri Rd.
- 14.9 Right onto S. Bay Blvd.
- 15.8 Morro Bay city limits.
- 16.1 Left into Morro Bay State Park.
- 16.3 Veer right onto Park View Dr., climbing up Black Hill to Black Hill Golf Course.
- 17.0 Summit at golf course.
- 17.2 Right out of park, onto Main St.
- 18.0 Left onto Marina.
- 18.1 Right onto Embarcadero.
- 18.5 Right onto Beach.
- 18.8 Left onto Main St.
- 19.2 Cross under Hwy. 1; continue straight on Main St.
- 19.7 Ride ends at Main St. and Hwy. 41.

Appendixes

A surprisingly large amount of literature is devoted to the sport of cycling. The following titles and club listings only begin to scratch the surface of what's out there, but they do provide a good starting place for learning more about all the various aspects of the sport. To really hook into California's vast cycling network in three easy steps, you should: 1. Join a local cycling club, 2. read *California Bicyclist* religiously, and 3. plan to complete at least one organized cycling event this year.

Regional Cycling Magazines

California Bicyclist
490 2nd St., Suite 304
San Francisco, CA 94107
(415) 546–7291

Publishes a Northern California and Southern California edition. This is the end-all-be-all source for bicycling news, events, and information in California. *California Bicyclist* publishes a complete calendar of events that is invaluable to anyone interested in cycling—recreational, touring, racing, or otherwise. It even publishes an annual *Pedalers' Guide,* which lists local cycling clubs throughout the state. You can get the magazine free at most bike shops, or purchase a subscription for $15.

City Sports
214 South Cedros Ave.
Solano Beach, CA 92075
(619) 793–2711

Competitor
214 South Cedros Ave.
Solano Beach, CA 92075
(619) 793–2711

Recommended Reading

Effective Cycling, John Forester, MIT Press. Tips for urban riding and for improving safe riding practices and skills.

Touring on Two Wheels, Dennis Coello, Nick Lyons Books. Practical information on safe and trouble-free bike touring.

Roadside Guide to Bike Repair, Dennis Coello, Warner Books.

Sloane's New Bicycle Maintenance Manual, Eugene Sloane, Simon & Schuster.

The Complete Book of Bicycling, Eugene Sloane, Simon & Schuster.

Off the Map: Bicycling Across Siberia, Mark Jenkins, William Morrow and Company. Eloquent and inspirational cycling travelogue—read this to renew your passion and enthusiasm for the sport.

The Outer Path: Finding My Way in Tibet, Jim Reynolds, Fair Oaks Publishing. Another great cycling travelogue.

How I Learned to Ride the Bicycle, Francis Willard, Fair Oaks Publishing. An American suffragette in the early 1900s tells of her experiences learning to ride "the wheel."

Tales from the Bike Shop, Maynard Hershon, Ten Speed Press. A collection of humorous short stories written by one of cycling's preeminent writers.

Short Bike Rides in and around Los Angeles, Bob Winning, Globe Pequot Press. Mostly urban rides in Los Angeles County.

Cycling San Diego, Jerry Schad and Nelson Copp, Centra Publications. Regional touring guide of San Diego County.

The Berkeley Guides: On the Loose in California, written by UC Berkeley students in cooperation with the Associated Students of the University of California, Fodors Travel Publications. My trusty companion during the writing of *The Best Bike Rides in California*, this book provides brutally honest travel information covering the entire state of California.

Cycling Maps

These maps were indispensable tools in the making of this book. Perhaps one day Krebs will have maps like these for the entire state!

Krebs Cycle Products, P.O. Box 7337, Santa Cruz, CA 95061
Lake Tahoe/Gold Country Bicycle Map
North San Francisco Bay/Sacramento Bicycle Touring Map
S.F. Peninsula/Santa Cruz Mountains Mountain Biking Map
South San Francisco Bay and Monterey Bay Area Bicycle Touring
    Map

On-Line Information

Cyclists with access to a computer and modem can hook up to the extensive Bike Net via America Online, where you can browse through hundreds of classifieds, sit in on live chats, and obtain a plethora of bike-related information. *Bicycling* magazine is also published on-line through America Online.

Cycling Clubs

National
League of American Wheel-
    men
190 West Ostend St., Suite 120
Baltimore, MD 21230
(301) 944–3399
National cycling club

Bikecentennial
P.O. Box 8308
Missoula, MT 59807
(406) 721–1776
National bike touring organiza-
tion; publishes cycling maps.

Regional
Cherry City Cyclists
P.O. Box 1972
San Leandro, CA 94577

Covina Cycling Club
Rideline: (818) 443–4353

Differnt Spokes
P.O. Box 14711
San Francisco, CA 94114

Fremont Freewheelers
P.O. Box 1089
Fremont, CA 94538

Fresno Cycling Club
P.O. Box 11531
Fresno, CA 93773

Grizzly Peak Cyclists
P.O. Box 9308
Berkeley, CA 94709

Orange County Wheelmen
P.O. Box 219
Tustin, CA 92681

Sacramento Wheelmen
920 27th Street
Sacramento, CA 95815

San Diego County Bicycle
    Coalition
P.O. Box 34544
San Diego, CA 92163
(619) 294–4916

Skyline Cycling Club
P.O. Box 60176
Sunnyvale, CA 94088

Stockton Bicycle Club
P.O. Box 4702
Stockton, CA 95204

Tailwinds Bicycle Club
P.O. Box 48
Santa Maria, CA 93456

Wandervogel
P.O. Box 252
Los Angeles, CA 90053–0252
(310) 295–3995
(714) 956–BIKE

Western Wheelers Bicycle
    Club
P.O. Box 518
Palo Alto, CA 94302

Westside Singles Cycling Club
Los Angeles
Hotline: (310) 364–4614

Credits

The quote on page 24 is from *How I Learned to Ride the Bicycle* by Francis Willard, copyright © 1991, Fair Oaks Publishing.

The quote on page 29 is from *Markings* by Dag Hammarskjöld, copyright © 1964, Knopf.

The quote on page 43 is from *My Work and Days* by Lewis Mumford, copyright © 1979, Harcourt Brace Jovanovich.

The quote on page 59 is from an article by Sean O'Faolain that appeared in the June 1958 issue of *Holiday*.

The quote on page 97 is from *Off the Map* by Mark Jenkins, copyright © 1992, William Morrow.

The quote on page 123 is from *Another Roadside Attraction* by Tom Robbins, copyright © 1992, Ballantine Books.

The quote on page 126 is from *The Portfolios of Ansel Adams* by Ansel Adams, copyright © 1981, New York Graphic Society/Little, Brown.

The quote on page 148 is from *The City is the Frontier* by Charles Abrams, copyright © 1965, Harper & Row.

The quote on page 153 is from an article by Bill Emerson that appeared in the July 29, 1967, issue of *The Saturday Evening Post.*

The quotes on pages 1, 10, 15, 49, 82, 106, and 169 are from various back issues of *California Bicyclist,* San Francisco. All quotes are reprinted with permission of the publisher.

About the Author

Kimberly Grob is the former editor of *California Bicyclist* magazine and regularly contributes to many national magazines including *Mountain Bike, Velo News, Women's Sports & Fitness, Backpacker, Inside Triathlon,* and *Triathlete.* She is an avid cyclist who dabbles in many aspects of the sport, including touring, mountain-bike racing, triathlon, and bike commuting. Kimberly lives in San Francisco and enjoys dashing through traffic on her mountain bike. She continues to dream of the day when she will be able to track-stand at a two-minute red light and ride as fast as the San Francisco bike messengers.

Best Bike Rides and Short Bike Rides

Here are the other fine titles offered in the Best Bike Rides and Short Bike Rides series, created for those who enjoy recreational cycling.

The Best Bike Rides in New England, $12.95
The Best Bike Rides in the Mid-Atlantic, $12.95
The Best Bike Rides in the Midwest, $12.95
The Best Bike Rides in the Pacific Northwest, $12.95
The Best Bike Rides in the South, $12.95

Short Bike Rides in and around Los Angeles, $11.95
Short Bike Rides in and around New York City, $9.95
Short Bike Rides in and around Philadelphia, $9.95
Short Bike Rides in and around San Francisco, $9.95
Short Bike Rides in and around Washington, D.C., $9.95
Short Bike Rides in Central and Western Massachusetts, $12.95
Short Bike Rides in Colorado, $10.95
Short Bike Rides in Connecticut, $9.95
Short Bike Rides in Eastern Massachusetts, $14.95
Short Bike Rides in Eastern Pennsylvania, $9.95
Short Bike Rides in Long Island, $8.95
Short Bike Rides in Michigan, $10.95
Short Bike Rides in New Jersey, $9.95
Short Bike Rides in Rhode Island, $10.95
Short Bike Rides in Western Washington, $12.95
Short Bike Rides on Cape Cod, Nantucket, Vineyard, $8.95

To order any of these titles with MASTERCARD or VISA, call toll-free (800) 243-0495; fax (800) 820-2329. Free shipping for orders of three or more books. Shipping charge of $3.00 per book for one or two books ordered. Connecticut residents add sales tax. Ask for a free catalogue of Globe Pequot's quality books on travel, nature, gardening, cooking, crafts, and more. Prices and availability subject to change.